WHAT COLOR IS
YOUR RETIREMENT?

The Life Options Guidebook to
Discover, Plan, and Live Your Retirement Dream

Richard P. Johnson, Ph.D.

Retirement Options
St. Louis, Missouri

What Color is Your Retirement?

Copyright © 2006 by Richard P. Johnson

ISBN 0-9743623-3-6

10 9 8 7 6 5 4 3 2
Second Edition – Jan. 2007

Cover design by Steve Gibbs

Printed in the United States of America

Contents

NOTICE

This book is designed to be used in conjunction with the LifeOptions Profile. The Profile offers a personal inventory of how prepared you are right now in the retirement success factors covered in this book. The Profile is an invaluable centerpiece for solid preparation and execution of a vital and vitalizing retirement phase of living life to the fullest. The LifeOptions Profile can only be administered through a certified Life Options Coach.

www.retirementoptions.com

INTRODUCTION

Grand and new opportunities are unfolding for those looking for successful transitions, the whole concept of retirement is dramatically changing. People are retiring earlier (average first retirement age is now 57.5) and often. Second and even third careers after one's first retirement are not at all uncommon. Labor participation of so-called "older workers" has been rising since the middle 1990s after years of steady decline. There are many forces behind this phenomenon but the inescapable fact is that many, if not most, retirees do in fact work after they retire. This might include you.

This "new retirement" includes a new definition of success, and a resurgence of a dream that may have been resident within us all along. For most of us, our work gave us a sense of ego-security knowing that we were "somebody;" that we were successful, at least at some level. Now we look for a new forum for success; we dream of a new challenge, a new meaning for us, and this yearning may raise a restlessness to pursue our dream in earnest.

1

What Color is Your Retirement?

We want change, but we may not quite know how to go about it. We dream of finding a better alignment, a more snug "fit," between our daily activities and our growing understanding of what's best for us now. We search for our dream, a place where we can expand our horizons. Here's where we begin assembling our dream, getting in touch with an image of personal success and meaning that is deeply satisfying, that goes beyond the boundaries of making a living. This journey into ourselves is key to the transition we call retirement.

This book is the companion for the LifeOptions Profile. The chapters herein align with the factors covered on the LifeOptions Profile. The personal information you receive on your LifeOptions Profile is extended and deepened in these pages so you can become ready for a life adventure unlike what has come before. If you haven't yet taken the LifeOptions Profile, I would like to invite you to do so as soon as you can. The personal data you will receive there has the power to bring your inner potential to more animated life.

Congratulations, and get ready for an exciting ride!

Richard P. Johnson, Ph.D.

Section One: Career & Work Arena

Introduction

It may seem strange indeed to begin a book on retirement by discussing work. Doesn't retirement mean stopping work? The answer is both *yes* and *no*. It's true that retirement means moving away from one's former work, but increasingly retirees are finding ways to either remain at work or are finding new work interests to satisfy something inside them.

The concept of work is universal in our culture; it's one of the first values we teach our children. We call this inclination to work our "work ethic." The work ethic tells us that working is "good" and not working isn't. This idea has been reinforced over and over throughout your life. For some people "just relaxing" is very difficult; they always seem to find something "to do," some project that needs finishing. Work so dominates their emotional make-up that they simply cannot settle down and enjoy any leisure time at all without having some little voice reminding them that they really should be accomplishing something "constructive."

Your perception of work in general determines the level of satisfaction you wish from work and the depth of meaning you expect from working. In addition, your view of work or what psychologists call your "work saliency" dictates whether you work in retirement at all, and what kind of work will suit you best in your post-retirement years. What do you want from work? Clarifying the roles and functions that you may want from work in your retirement will assist you in making more accurate work decisions and vastly increase your confidence during your retirement transition.

We all give different value to working. For some of us we *need* to work to feel ourselves; others can't wait for the time when they can simply relax or play all day long. Getting a grip on your work preferences is a central issue for you during this retirement preparation time.

Chapter One

Ideal Work: Discovering Your Personal Dream for Tomorrow

I once heard retirement described as: *following your dream*! Wouldn't you like to be able to translate your dream into reality in your retirement? You can if you know what your Ideal Work might be. Yes, retirement is about getting away from work, but it's also about getting 'in touch' with those activities that give you a sense of fulfillment. Finding activities that satisfy you personally is a central task for all of us who are approaching retirement, regardless of how we might view retirement right now. We want to create something of an ideal for ourselves in retirement. This gets us to your ideal work; chances are that you'll be doing some type of work, even if you don't call it work, in your retirement.

Work and Personality

Everyone has a unique personality. There are over 6.5 billion people who live on this earth, and no two of them are identical. Your personality shines brighter when you're with certain people, in certain settings, and in certain kinds of activities. The more aware you are of your personality the better you'll be able to select activities in your retirement that bring you the most satisfaction.

The esteemed career developmentalist John Holland devised a simple yet quite effective framework of six personalities that provide us with a good starting point for identifying the kinds of activities that might bring us the most satisfaction. Holland connected these six categories, or work personality types, together, and then harnessed them to specific work activities and skills. Here they are:

1. The <u>REALISTIC</u> Personality Type: People who like to move their body in their work activities. They like the manual skilled jobs; they like being athletic. They prefer to work with objects, machines, tools, plants, or animals; they generally prefer the outdoors.

    a. <u>Manual Skills</u>: Molding, shaping, preparing, assembling, setting-up, moving, shipping, handling, precision work, washing, cooking, cleaning, fitting, adjusting, tuning, producing.

    b. <u>Athletic/Outdoor/Traveling Skills</u>: General sports skills, competition, creating, planning, coordinating outdoor activities, cultivating, growing things, working with animals.

2. The <u>CONVENTIONAL</u> Personality Type: People who like to work with data, and/or have clerical or

numerical ability. They like carrying things out in detail or following through on other's instructions. They tend to like guidelines and specific operating procedures. They even read directions!

a. Detail and Follow through Skills: Implementing, getting things done, bringing the project in on time, finding ways to speed-up the job, good at getting materials, keeping confidences, detail person, keeps good records, organized.

b. Numerical/Financial/Accounting skills: Ability with numbers, taking inventory, managing money, appraising, budget planning, preparing financial reports, logical.

3. The ENTERPRISING Personality Type: People who like to work with other people, especially in influencing them, persuading them, and leading or managing them to reach goals for personal or economic gain.

a. Influencing/Persuading skills: Develop rapport and trust, persuade, promote, recruiting talent, arbitrate, mediate, manipulate.

b. Performing skills: Getting before a group, demonstrating showmanship, playing music, making people laugh, acting, and public sports.

c. Leadership skills: Initiating, driving, good time management, promoting and bringing about change, showing courage, solving problems, motivating others, directing creative talent.

   <u>d.</u> <u>Developing/Planning/Organizing/</u>
<u>Supervising/Management skills</u>:
Planning, projecting, prioritizing, organizing,
scheduling, assigning, directing others,
responsibility, attaining, reviewing.

4. The <u>SOCIAL</u> Personality Type: People who like to work with other people informing them, enlightening them, helping them, training them, developing them, healing or curing them. They are generally quite skilled with words ... they can describe things very well.

   a. <u>Language/Reading/Writing/Speaking/Com-</u>
<u>municating skills</u>: Reading, composing,
defining, translating, summarizing, and
outstanding writing skills.
   b. <u>Instructing/Interpreting/Guiding/</u>
<u>Educational skills</u>: Knowledgeable, explaining,
coaching, conveying, encouraging,
communicating effectively, facilitating personal
growth, empowering.
   c. <u>Serving/Helping/Human Relationships</u>:
Servicing, rendering, sensitivity to others,
listening, attentively, good human relations,
caring, nursing, mentoring, expert in liaison
roles.

5. The <u>ARTISTIC</u> Personality Type: People who have artistic, innovating, or intuitional preferences. They like to work in unstructured situations, using their imagination or creativity.

a. Intuitional and Innovating skills: Imaging, idea producing, innovation, synthesizing, seeing relationships, updating, applying theory.

b. Artistic skills: Expressing love of beauty, good sense of humor, creative imaging, visualizing concepts, designing, musical knowledge and tasks.

6. The INVESTIGATIVE Personality Type: People who like to find things out, discover things, analyze things, evaluate data, and solve problems.

a. Observational Learning skills: Observing, skillful listening, appraising, assessing.

c. Research / Investigation / Analyzing / Systemizing/ Evaluating skills: Anticipating problems, surveying, analyzing, diagnosing, grouping, testing, finding-out, evaluating, decision making.

You don't have to exhibit every skill listed in any particular set to feel that you've identified your most prominent category or 'work personality,' you need only feel that the majority of those listed apply to you in general. The more skill sets you identify as your own, the better you'll be able to broaden your horizons in your next life phase.

> **NOTE: Look under the "Career & Work" Arena on page four (4) of your LifeOptions Profile where you'll find how you ranked these six work personalities.**

What Color is Your Retirement?

Your personal dream for tomorrow may be continuing with the same work personality that you favored in the past. On the other hand, you may decide that you've had enough of that and you now want to change. For many, the dream that our work could bring us full and ultimate happiness fades as we approach retirement and prepare for our next life step. Retirement offers you the life-balancing option of expressing a side of yourself you never exercised before, and so we observe the accountant who built his own vacation house in retirement, the teacher who went into farming, the executive who decided to enter politics, the truck driver who took up teaching, and many more. Chances are that these retirees were following their dreams; a dream that lay fallow during their working years, and now can emerge and stretch its wings.

Dreams are necessary; they give us hope and a purpose for living, a direction, a course of action that offers order and harmony to our lives. In retirement we find this dream escaping from its hiding place within us and making itself known.

> Your dream offers you the brightest hope that there is more of you yet to become.

Pieces of your retirement dream may surface in a night or daydream; or your dream may pierce the surface of your consciousness when you're thoughtlessly engaged in some everyday activity. You can retrieve your dream or reject it, ponder it or push it away, but the dream lingers within you. Your dream may not be a grand scheme of adventure that will forever change the course of humankind, but your dream leads your journey toward deeper personal authenticity. Make no mistake that you have a dream, and that your dream seeks expression. Your dream will not rest until you give it some exposure in your life. Our retirement challenge is to discover our dream and then to translate it into some type of ideal work/activity in retirement.

We all long to taste the sweetness of living out our dream. Perhaps your dream will never unfold completely in your life, yet it's in your retirement years when the question of your personal dream seems to reassert itself with renewed vigor. It is at this time when we come to realize more fully that we've invested the lion's share of our life energy into building our identity around our occupation. Now that retirement is on the horizon, this energy expenditure needs some realignment and perhaps even redefinition.

> **In the 10-year period between 2000 and 2010 the population of men aged 55-64 will increase by 47.2%; for women it increases 46.6%.** *Bureau of Labor Statistics*

What Color is Your Retirement?

Chapter Two
Work Benefits

Most of us have worked for the greater part of our life. Over the years work has given us several benefits that have become such integral parts of our lives that they have raised themselves to the level of "needs." A need is something that has become a *requirement*; if we don't satisfy this requirement, we will begin to lose ourselves in some ways, and could ultimately get sick.

We must find replacements for each of these five benefits of work if we are to live fully in retirement. These five are:

1. **Financial Compensation:** The first long-standing work benefit, and now retirement need, is financial compensation that enables us to meet our material needs. Usually this takes the form of a paycheck. Unfortunately, many persons look only to replace their income benefit as they prepare for retirement. This myopia may blind them to the fact that there

13

are four other benefits/needs they must also somehow satisfy in retirement as well.

2. **Time Management:** The second work benefit is time management. Our work gives our life structure; it manages our time. Some would say that their work over-manages their time, or even commands their time. The fact remains that our work usually lets us know what we will be doing next Monday morning. The time management function keeps our life orderly and somehow "in-sync" with the beat of the culture around us.

3. **Sense of Utility:** The third benefit of our work is to give us a sense of utility or purpose. Having purpose injects a feeling of meaning into our life. Our work offers us tasks that are needed in our society; somebody needs this work accomplished to such a degree that they are willing to pay you for your services to do it. We feel a sense of contribution; we know that we are useful ... we have utility ... we are of worth to others by bringing value or serving their needs.

4. **Status:** The fourth work benefit is status. It is from our work that we accrue a certain status in our community. We have a definite place in the schema of the world. Status is not haughty or self-serving; it is not competitive, nor is it condescending. Rather, status is that combined sense of personal worth and identity we derive from

knowing who and what we are. Each job in our culture has a certain status attached to it.

5. **Socialization:** Finally, our work brings us in very close, if not constant contact with many other people; this is socialization. We interact with others, we develop relationships, form friendships, and learn how to cooperate at higher and higher levels as our increasingly complex work places demand higher and higher levels of coordination, connection, intercommunication, and interaction.

NOTE: Look at page four (4) of your LifeOptions Profile where you'll find your "Work Benefits" score – red, yellow, or green.

These five benefits do not go away simply because we retire; they have become a part of us to such a degree that we cannot simply discard them without some emotional, psychological, and even spiritual consequences. How many times have we heard of, or seen for ourselves, persons who were formerly very involved, even consumed with their work, emotionally "crash" sometime after they retire? Usually it's not because of some sudden catastrophic event like running out of money, or losing their home. More commonly it's a slow wearing away of the individual; it's the unseen losses that gradually push us out of balance. We're not quite ourselves; we may get easily out of sorts, or just feel a sense of being somewhat down. In more extreme instances we may feel a sense of personal fragmentation that can even escalate into depression if left unaddressed. One or more of these five may be at the heart of our discontent. It's crucial that these five work benefits are replaced in some way as we transition toward retirement.

Chapter Three
Work Options

Many retirees, if not most, continue working in some fashion or capacity after they retire; they find ways of replacing the five benefits that they formerly received from their full time paid working career. The U.S. Dept. of Labor defines a person as "retired" if, 1) you work less than full time, and 2) some portion of your income comes from a pension, or pension-like vehicle. Being retired certainly doesn't mean that you don't work. So, what are your thoughts about working in your retirement years?

Here are the latest Dept. of Labor, Bureau of Labor Statistics numbers on labor force participation of "older workers." All numbers are as of 2000.

What Color is Your Retirement?

MEN

Age	% working	full time	part time
55-61	71.3%	92.3%	7.7%
62-64	47.1	77.9	22.1
65-69	30.4	60.5	39.5
70+	12.3	48.5	51.5

WOMEN

Age	% working	full time	part time
55-61	50.8%	77.2%	22.8%
62-64	34.6	61.3	38.7
65-69	19.8	44.2	55.8
70+	5.9	36.4	63.6

The average age of first retirement in the United Stated stands at 57.5 years old. It's easy to see then that many retirees do indeed work after they retire. Almost half (47.1%) of all men between the ages of 62 and 64 are working; of that number, 77.9% are working full time, and 22.1% are working part time. These are significant numbers! Almost one third (30.4%) of all men between the ages of 65 to 69 are working; 60.5% of them work full time, while 39.5% work part time. The figures for women are a bit lower but still in the same direction as the men. These numbers are even more surprising since the over 65 group receives full social security benefits.

And while many are still working, here's a breakdown of where retirement income comes from:

<u>Retirement Income for Those Aged 65+ (1998)</u>

- From Earnings 20.7%
- Social Security 37.6%
- Employer Benefits 18.7%
- Personal Assets 19.9%
- Other 3.1%

TOTAL   100% of income

So why are retirees choosing to either stay working or, more the case, find other employment? Many forces can motivate retirees to keep working. First of course is finances. Some retirees simply need the money to pay bills; others need to work to help their children financially, still others remain at work to receive medical benefits that are either unaffordable or unavailable privately. Some retirees return to work after being "down-sized," "right-sized," or in some way "spun-out" of their positions. These folks feel somewhat vocationally displaced since they're out of work earlier than they had intended.

Another factor keeping people working is that they are simply healthier and can continue to exert themselves longer at older ages than we've previously seen. Finally, a factor that is difficult to get any "hard" data on is retirees returning to work because they feel that without working they feel somewhat lost, they simply want something to do, and/or because they find retirement unfulfilling. We'll cover this more later in the "Personal Development" section of this book.

Options for Working in Retirement

If you even entertain the possibility that you might plan on working in your retirement, what form might this work take? Here are eight work options for working in retirement. There is no one formula for success in retirement as every retiree is different.

1. Full time work in the same general field as your pre-retirement work.
2. Full time work in a field other than what you do/did before retirement.
3. Half time work (20 hours or so per week)
4. Part time work (less than 20 per week)
5. Self-employment of some kind.
6. Become a consultant.
7. Volunteer work only.
8. Mix of volunteer and paid work.

NOTE: Look on page 4 in your Life Options Profile where you'll find your top three retirement work preferences.

Resources

Job Search/Career Change

Monster.com
http://careersat50.monster.com/

AARP > Money & Work > Careers
http://www.aarp.org/money/careers/

Senior Job Bank
http://www.seniorjobbank.com/

Seniors4Hire
http://www.seniors4hire.org/

What Color is Your Parachute?
http://www.jobhuntersbible.com/

Retirement Jobs
http://www.retirementjobs.com/

Holland Career
http://www.hollandcodes.com/
John Holland's website. Learn a lot here and take any of his
assessments, including the *Self-Directed Search*

Career Counselor
http://www.nbcc.org/counselorfind2 National Board of
Certified Counselors --- Find a counselor in your area who
specializes in career help.

Retirement Coach
http://www.retirementoptions.com Find a certified retirement
coach in your area. Click on *Find A Coach.*

Owning a Business
Startup Journal from the Wall Street Journal
http://www.startupjournal.com/

Entreprenuer.com
http://www.entrepreneur.com/

SCORE (Service Corps of Retired Executives)
http://www.score.org/

Inc.com
http://www.inc.com/

U.S. Small Business Administration (SBA) > Starting Your
Business
http://www.sba.gov/starting_business/

Suggested Readings
"7 Fundamental Rules for Crafting a Rock-Solid Resume"
"8 Interview Questions for Older Workers"
"10 Job Ideas for Older Workers"
AARP Bulletin, Sept 2002, by Lance Helgeson

Dictionary of Holland Occupational Codes
The DHOC contains descriptions of occupations and estimates of
interests and aptitudes associated with each occupation according to
the six occupational classifications by John Holland described in the
Ideal Work section. www.parinc.com
Occupational Outlook Handbook
Find out lots about every job in America: significant points, nature of
the work, working conditions, employment, training, job outlook,
earnings, related occupations, and sources of additional information.
You can access it at http://www.bls.gov/oco/

Section Two: Health & Wellness Arena
Introduction

Your **Health & Wellness Arena** consists of all the energy that you expend helping your body and your mind work as healthfully as possible. We are each in-charge of the care and maintenance of our body, and our own mental attitude. This arena includes how you maintain your physical health, how you relate to yourself internally and how you discipline yourself physically and mentally.

THREE LEVELS OF WELLNESS

Wellness is an all-encompassing notion that includes finding fulfillment on three levels of human living. The first level is *physical well-being*, which we simply call <u>well</u>. The second level of wellness is *mental wellness*, which we call <u>wise</u>. The third level of wellness involves finding *personal meaning* in your life, which we call <u>whole</u>. At every life step and stage, we seek to become, and remain well, wise, and whole. This is particularly important in retirement, for in these years we grow into a level of maturation necessary to really "get a grip" on these three aspects of wellness.

- **Well** = Physical Well-Being
- **Wise** = Mental Wellness
- **Whole** = Personal Meaning

Each of these levels of human functioning requires special skills that together contribute mightily to your wellness and well-being in retirement.

Each of the three chapters in this section covers a unique component of the total "package" of what it means to be optimally well. These three chapters are:

Chapter 4	**Health Practices**
Chapter 5	**Vitality**
Chapter 6	**Your Wellness Attitudes**

Chapter Four
Health Practices

Retirees need a physical fitness plan; they need guidelines that can help make their retirement dream a reality. Retirees, who actively pursue this goal, like the feeling of knowing that they are doing what is necessary to keep the marvelous machine of their body in top running condition.

There are seven health practices that together allow retirees to perform maximally. These practices serve as the foundation for wellness, the backdrop for vitality.

1. <u>Avoid tobacco use</u>. Tobacco has little, if any place in the life of a maturing person seeking lifespan vitality. The research is done, the data is in; there is no question that any type of tobacco use is clearly harmful to one's health. While it is true that some persons seem to have a higher tolerance to tobacco than others, it is indisputable that tobacco has detrimental effects upon all those who use it regardless of their genetic make-up and tobacco sensitivity.

2. <u>Proper nutrition</u>: More, and more, and still more research arrives each day extolling the virtues of constructive dietary modifications. Somehow we all know to eat a balanced diet, to include at least five fruits and/or vegetables every day, to ingest 6 to 8 glasses of water every day, to moderate our salt intake, to watch fats and oils, curb our use of red meat, etc, etc. Yet, just because we know that these dietary habits are very useful, how many of us can say that we regularly follow them?

3. <u>Positive response to stress</u>: Each of us feels distress in different ways. What may be distress for some is actually a motivating challenge for others. We need to know our stressors and to devise constructive and healthful measures to manage them, even convert them into life enhancers.

4. <u>Sufficient sleep and relaxation</u>: Some researchers maintain that since the invention of the light bulb, and especially since the advent of television, we have become a nation of sleep-deprived individuals. Sleep is rejuvenating, relaxing, and physically necessary. Each of us needs slightly different amounts of sleep, but we all need adequate sleep. Mature adults monitor their "sleep need" requirements and insure that they get what they need.

5. <u>Maintaining ideal weight</u>: Obesity is perhaps the most disturbing risk factor in our culture. Fast food, rich food, fatty food, and too much food all add inches to our waistlines, subtract years from our lives, and rob us of vitality.

6. Moreover use of alcohol: Recent research indicates that one-ounce of alcohol per day for most persons is beneficial to their health. Yet, let's not make the mistake of thinking that since a little is good, a lot is definitely better. Over two ounces of alcohol per day, for the average person, begins damaging the body rather than assisting it. The damage can be generalized, affecting all systems of the body; it can also be localized, as in inhibited liver function. Alcohol is also a depressant, and can over the long haul, deprive you of your natural bodily and emotional rhythms; it can disrupt your mood and even trigger anger.

7. Sufficient exercise: Our bodies need ample amounts of exercise. Research indicates that 20 to 30 minutes of vigorous exercise three to four times per week is necessary to keep our bodies in good conditioning. Naturally, some persons, due to many factors, cannot exercise vigorously the way they would want. Nonetheless, some exercise is almost always possible and needs to be pursued.

SELF-HEALTH CARE SKILLS

The bottom line of healthy living is that we must care for ourselves. *Wellness has clear attitudinal qualities; wellness is not simply the absence of disease.*

Self-health care responsibility means learning and practicing skills that aid your health and wellness. There are four main skills to master:

1. Assertiveness: Assertiveness means being able to clearly state what you need and what you want to achieve optimal

health. Part of assertiveness is to "own" your own needs, communicate these needs to those who needs to know, and then actively work to incorporate these needs into reality.

2. <u>Establish Priorities:</u> Some things are simply more important than others; our health and wellness needs to be very high on our priority list. We live best when we are healthy. Living a healthy life requires our active participation. We need to live our lives as a connoisseur, choosing each task, each food, each behavior with great care and consideration.

3. <u>Learn how to live a relaxed lifestyle:</u> Living a relaxed lifestyle means more than being leisurely, it means becoming as centered as possible, as mindful of one's presence in the moment as possible. Developing such a perspective frees us from the tyranny of thinking we are not doing enough for our selves and for our health.

4. <u>Develop a new attitude about discomfort:</u> Discomfort is felt at a subjective level, no one feels discomfort exactly like you do. Some persons learn to live with a level of discomfort that would completely hobble another person. This may be the discomfort of gastric upset, or arthritis pain, or emotional pain, or joint stiffness, or any of a vast array of physical imperfections that we encounter as a result of living. Discomfort is part of living. There exists no discomfort-free state of existence on this earth. To what degree can you shift your perspective about the many discomforts in your life away from discomfort causing debilitation and toward functionality?

Chapter Five
Vitality

Who among us doesn't want to remain well and fit for as long as we can? We hear so much about longevity enhancement today for mature adults, yet aren't we actually more interested in investing the years we've been given with as much vitality as possible, rather than simply extending our years? When we invest in vitality enhancement measures, we are at the same time investing in long life development as well.

Vitality is akin to wellness, but much more immediate. Wellness is the backdrop for vitality, and can be conceived of as a state of living fully, finding maximum fulfillment from all areas of life: your occupation, family, finances, relationships, education, spirit, and of course, your body.

Wellness is **not** simply the absence of disease. Health is a very personal thing, a state of thriving not simply surviving. Some have put it very clearly when they say that wellness means adding life to your years, not simply years to your life!

What Color is Your Retirement?

Vitality means living life with zest and energy, savoring life, enjoying life, relishing it, injecting vibrancy into everything we do. Vitality is a personal concept; we each pursue it differently. Some retirees find vitality by pursuing as active a lifestyle as they can; others find vitality by being more contemplative. Whatever strategy you choose will work for you as long as you feel you are expressing your true nature in a genuine way, and that you are aware that you are living vitally in the present moment. Perhaps the biggest part of vitality is awareness that we are living vitally right now. You can't live with vitality yesterday or tomorrow...only today!

Vitality must be real, not contrived or put-on. It's much too easy in our sensationalizing and faultfinding world to take on a defeatist attitude about life in general. Such an attitude separates us from others, and alienates us even from ourselves. A defeatist attitude is like poison to our vitality. With all the forces that seem to be tearing us down in our modern world, it's more important than ever to make vitality enhancement, living fully, and living positively, our top personal priority.

The Ten Points of Vitality

Here are ten descriptors of retirees who live life with vitality.

1. <u>Has a high self-regard</u>: They seem to think favorable about themselves even in the face of trial and tribulation. They harbor an internal sense of "all

30

rightness" at their core that appears undisturbed by outside pressures. Certainly they can become upset and irritable at times, but they regain composure rather quickly and emerge without damage to their self.

2. Value their physical health: They monitor their body and are aware of its needs. They are kind to their body in the sense that they don't overtax it, they give it proper rest, grooming, exercise, medical attention, etc. They have realistic expectations about what is appropriate for them at their stage of life.

3. Have a high sense of personal worth: They see themselves as valuable; they recognize their accomplishments as successes, and can easily understand how useful their work is to the overall project. They enjoy a high sense of utility; they believe that what they are doing is worthwhile.

4. Have faith in themselves: They understand at deep levels that they are capable, resourceful, and enduring. They enjoy an appropriate sense of personal confidence, which is seldom, if ever, overstated. They seem to possess an aura of stability and security.

5. Expect success: They have a hard time believing in failure. What other people might call failure, they seem to recognize as just another learning experience. They expect good things to happen right from the outset of a project or task.

31

6. Enjoy productive and supportive relationships: Perhaps because of their internal confidence, they enjoy people. They don't fear that they will be unfairly criticized, and if someone does become upset with them, they can handle the situation with appropriate social skill.

7. Take optimal care of their body: They like the feeling of knowing that they are doing what is necessary to keep the marvelous machine of their body in top running condition. They feed it correctly, get proper rest, maintain a regular exercise program, and perform other health maintenance and promotion activities, which allow them to perform maximally.

8. Engage in stress reduction techniques: Whether it's regular exercise, mindfulness meditation, progressive muscle relaxation, a power nap, prayer, soothing music, appropriate "self-talk," or any of a number of other stress reduction techniques; they know several and use them regularly.

9. Take good care of all their gifts: They know their gifts and talents as an individual, and maintain an active interest in the development and growth of their talents. They seem to appreciate what they have been given and are not particularly envious of the talents and gifts of others.

10. Make continuous adjustments to their attitudes and behaviors: They seem to know innately that their attitudes are the bedrock of their personality and that

they need to keep on top of which ones need modification and in what ways these modifications can be made. Attitudes can become antiques, useful yesterday, but quite out of function today. Sometimes we neglect to trade-in our antique attitudes for newer, more functional models.

> *Vitality means injecting the present moment with its full measure of life and love.*

Vitality means searching for the spark that exists right here, right now! Vitality is proactive, productive, positive, and spontaneous without being impulsive. Vitality means living to the fullest extent possible, under whatever conditions are presented to you. Vitality means finding the luster that exists in each and every situation: finding the love, finding the miracle. Vitality means grabbing the "gusto" that's always there.

Vital living depends very little on the outside and is almost entirely dependent upon one's internal world. Even persons who are sick can find vitality in their lives despite their hampered lifestyle, as well as can persons in robust health. Persons living in a less than enhancing relationship can live with vitality, as can persons who live in a blissful relationship. Vitality is not blind to the circumstances of one's life, but vitality can be the force to help us look at what enhances us rather than what tears us down.

Vitality Blockers

Vitality emerges naturally in a person as a mindset of living fully is progressively developed, and when potential wellness obstacles (or blockers) are removed. The following vitality blockers can prevent you from experiencing genuine vitality, and thus living fully. Dr. Norman Shealy, M.D. and Caroline Myss say in their book, The Creation of Health, (Stillpoint Publishing, 1993) that people can accelerate illness when one or more of the following eight dysfunctional patterns are present:

1. The presence of unresolved or deeply consuming emotional, psychological or spiritual stress in your life. Chief among such vitality blockers are: holding a grudge, unresolved grief or anger, unexpressed feelings, resentments, injustices, abuse, and/or neglect.

2. The degree of influence that negative belief patterns have upon a person's reality. Your beliefs are the "mother" of your actions. We can, without even knowing it, hold on to beliefs that are "antiques," they had utility at one time in your life, but have now lost their utility.

3. The inability to give or receive love. We all have the need to both receive and to give love. When either of these is blocked we "set ourselves up" for

illness. Since these are "needs" this means that without fulfillment, at some level, we <u>will</u> get sick.

4. Lack of humor and the inability to distinguish serious concerns from the lesser issues of life. It's been said that the most happy people are ones who "don't sweat the small stuff in life and who believe that everything is small stuff." We do need to gain the perspective that human behavior can sometimes "go over the top." Instead of getting angry at it, humor allows us to find it amusing.

5. How effectively one exercises the power of choice. So often we don't recognize that we <u>do</u> have the power of choice; we have options. I'm always amazed at the number of intelligent persons who simply can't accept this notion. If we don't have options, if we don't have choices, then we are all trapped.

6. How well a person has attended to the needs of the physical body itself; i.e., nutrition, exercise, genetic makeup, and use of drugs or alcohol. As the last lesson clearly pointed out, we can misuse our body only so far, and for so long before our body gives us rather clear and unpleasant signals that all is not well.

7. How one has dealt with the "existential vacuum" or the suffering that accompanies the absence or loss of meaningful things in one's life. This is

particularly true for some mature adults who formerly had positions of great responsibility or clear personal significance leading to above average personal meaning, only to suffer the loss of this meaning through retirement, either chosen or otherwise.

8. The characteristics of people who become ill because of a tendency toward denial or circumstances or events that must be changed. Change is the watchword of the universe. All things must and do change. We also change, unfortunately some of us cannot change ourselves, and we simply let circumstances make our change decisions for us. This ensures pain and suffering, if not for us, then for others.

Chapter Six

Wellness Attitudes

How much are you "in-charge" of your health? How much are you "in charge" of your wellness? Are these two ideas the same? How are they different?

Your attitudes about your health and your well-being did not suddenly flash into your mind; they were formed over time, since you were a child. Your parents particularly had an immense impact upon your attitudes about yourself and how to care for yourself, as well as your self-esteem.

Medical researchers have studied the interactions between psychological factors and the functioning of the immune system. The immune system wards off bodily invaders such a viruses, bacteria, and other pathogens. Their findings indicate that healthy maturing adults have just as good immune system functioning as persons half their age. But the startling

37

fact uncovered is that our attitudes about ourselves and about life in general has a direct impact upon how our bodies ward off disease and discomfort.

Your attitudes and beliefs about wellness & well-being can have dramatic effects upon the actual physical functioning of your body. Constructive thinking and positive feelings do improve your health. Positive thinking translates into a healthier immune system functioning, while negative thinking does just the opposite. The choice is actually yours to make. Do you want to give your body messages that say "live" or "die?"

Health is a very personal thing,
strive for a state of thriving not simply surviving.

THE NECESSITY FOR CHANGE

Change of course is necessary over your entire lifespan. There is never a time when change is not a mandatory ingredient in a person's life. This fact becomes even more important for us as we mature. We experience changes in our health status, our relationship with our bodies, and our own sense of who we are. Paradoxically, it's normal as we mature to slightly shift emphasis away from our body while at the same time needing to focus more (not less) attention onto our health needs.

Yet it seems only a small percentage of maturing persons genuinely and proactively strive to make the lifestyle changes necessary so optimal health and wellness can be maintained for as long as possible. Some retirees try to ignore the necessary changes in lifestyle, others actively resist these changes.

When we resist change we inadvertently set ourselves up for some form of pain. Sooner or later the balancing mechanisms within us aren't readjusted and we gradually begin slipping into some form of ill-health. This can take many forms; emotional, relational, physical or even in our spirit.

Self-Health Care Factors

What are the factors that allow some individuals to seek responsibility for their own health and wellness, while others seem confined to inactivity? Why is it that some adults seem quite eager to take action in a dependable manner so that they can make healthy lifestyle changes, while others seem stagnant? Why do some individuals quite naturally and smoothly assume health seeking behaviors, and have a sustained motivation for their own health, while others seem quite "health asleep?" The first step toward positive self-health care responsiveness is the awareness and understanding of health promotion behaviors.

> *"How old would you be if you didn't know your age?"*
> Satchel Paige

PERSONALITY AND SELF-HEALTH CARE

One thing we know for sure is that as persons mature they become more different from one and other. As personal history nudges us, and environmental changes push us, family structure, occupational diversity, genetic make-up, and thousands of other factors converge over time and interact with our unique personality to create the distinct "YOU" that you are today. There are many ways to address personality differences, however the *Berkeley Growth Study* classifications of the five styles of retirement living align well with self-health responsiveness.

1. **Mature**: A mature personality is one that takes self-health care seriously in the sense that these persons value their health and wellness as a clear priority. They treat themselves as responsible adults. They shoulder the actions necessary for constructive modifications in their lifestyle and see themselves as good choice makers. They generate alternatives and seek responsibility for making wellness happen. In short, they foster change in their lives.

2. **Rocking Chair**: A rocking chair personality believes that their retirement years are for resting. They take notice of their health only when pressed by stark discomfort to do so. They are passive in their responsiveness toward behavioral modifications that could improve, enrich, or enhance their health. They seem to live by the adage, "What will be, will be."

3. **Armored**: The armored personality is rather "up tight" about her or his health. They may be constantly vigilant about what could be going wrong with their body. They tend to over-react to discomfort and tend to consult professional

health care providers more than necessary. They over-define their health, may overdo exercise, dieting, and so forth.

4. **Depressed**: The depressed personality (which has many forms) causes people to either inflate their health concerns or do just the opposite, and deflate them. In their search for reasons why they feel badly, they may imagine their bodies are malfunctioning when actually they are physically fine. They may become somewhat hypochondriacal, i.e., thinking they are sick when they are not. On the other hand, they may feel so badly that they neglect their health.

5. **Angry**: The angry personality generally shuns professional health care in deference to their own. Rather than seeing their overall health and wellness as a partnership between themselves and professional health care providers, they discount and even distrust professionals and consequently shoulder their health management by themselves, only consulting professionals when something traumatic occurs.

Which retirement personality are you headed for?

BLOCKERS OF SELF-HEALTH CARE RESPONSIVENESS

1. Belief in myths about maturation and health

Somewhere in our culture's quest for the holy grail of health, we may find ourselves with a dangerous belief that quality health care is measured in terms of the quantity of health care we receive. This belief may be said to have penetrated so deeply into our minds that it borders on a myth, something we believe that simply isn't true.

Another health care myth is that we must <u>receive</u> health care from professionals in all situations, rather than be more selective of those times when it would be most prudent giving it to oneself. Such a notion seems to defer the responsibility for your health to the "wisdom" of your medical caregivers. Certainly, we must place our trust in the knowledge and the competencies of our health caregivers, yet we can carry this notion out to a most illogical extension when we somehow unknowingly assume that our health care is their responsibility, not our own.

Both these myths can work against our quest for optimal health. They have special impact upon the lives of maturing adults who, as a group interact more frequently with the medical care community than other age groups. When these two myths become embedded into our belief core we can almost completely *relinquish* our health care to health care professionals. Such a situation invades the psychological sense of self that is required for optimal functioning, and robs you of self-care decision making.

2. Erroneous expectations and perceptions of health

Perhaps the biggest expectation about health and wellness that acts as a stumbling block for maturing adults is the momentum of their previous lifestyle. We somehow frame our health in terms of what it was yesterday; "My health was fine yesterday, so it will be today and tomorrow as well." Such a health perspective only blocks positive and necessary change. Because we were healthy yesterday we keep the same eating, exercise, lifestyle, sleep patterns, etc. that we used yesterday. We become blind to the need for lifestyle and attitudinal change.

3. Distorted thinking about self-health care

Our thinking includes our assessments, our opinions, and our judgments about health and the mix between self-care and professional care. Our thinking can bring us down a path where we over-rely on professional health care personnel, with the thought, "I really shouldn't take care of myself medically." On the other hand our thinking may do the opposite. We may over-inflate the value of our own self-health care, like the woman who thought she could treat the lump in her breast solely with mega doses of vitamin E.

4. Dispirited feelings about self-health care

Dispirited feelings refer to a sense of insufficiency or inadequacy of self which leads to over relying on professional health care professionals. "I'm not good enough," or "I can never do the right thing" and other such feelings about one's own effectiveness can hamper self-health care behavior.

5. Decision blocks

We need information to make the kind of considered choices regarding health care that lead to the desired outcomes.

For maturing adults, facing physical changes as never before, the array of alternatives may seem mammoth indeed. The only alternative that seems likely is to seek professional assistance; and clearly that may be the wisest choice in most cases; but certainly not all.

FACTORS OF
SELF-HEALTH CARE RESPONSIVENESS

Personal responsibility starts with self-awareness and heightened awareness of *oneself.* As our body changes, so do the needs of that body. Some of these needs become more obvious as we mature; decreased sensitivity of all five senses, lowered strength and speed of reaction time, need for strength training, need for pacing, more need for rest. Other physical needs are not as clear: nutrition and hydration modifications, stature and flexibility changes, gradual wearing of joints, chronic hypertension, metabolic changes, medication interaction incidents, gradual sleep quality interruptions, exercise requirements, and a host of others.

These changes call for a new level of self-health care responsibility. This responsibility includes many factors. Consider the following factors:

1. <u>A renewed commitment to the issue of health</u>. As the body matures we are forced to give it more, not less attention. Modifications of all sorts are necessary. Most of us have sustained an injury of some dimension in our lives and have experienced the need to make temporary shifts in the way

we do things. Others have had surgery and the requisite need
for recuperation and even physical rehabilitation. Yet the
specter of physical modifications on a more or less permanent
basis may send shock waves through us as never before.

2. <u>Conscious intention to make the environment of life
better as we mature</u>. Many persons blessed with robust health
may pay scant attention to their health. Their bodies have
always responded very well to all the demands. Consequently,
such persons may be unprepared for the modifications in self-
health care necessary as the maturation process progresses.
Other adults simply deny that changes are taking place and may
unconsciously take steps to either cover-up or simply side step
the necessary modifications.

3. <u>Engagement in the preparation steps necessary to
smooth the way toward improved or sustained health</u>. Once
your health consciousness has been sufficiently raised, and you
develop a firm intention to address your own health from a
more formal standpoint, it's then time to begin developing
options for improved health on a physical level. Many persons
seem dumbfounded when asked to generate self-health care
options that could raise their overall level of wellness. Yet we
can't hope to actually change our lives until we have some
options in order to make accurate choices.

4. <u>Involvement or participation in the work necessary
to make improved or sustained health a reality</u>. This means we
actually need to take some action. Action may be the biggest
obstacle facing so many maturing adults. Let's try to break this
action step down a bit.

SELF-HEALTH CARE MOTIVATION

Some years ago the world famous distance runner Jim Fixx died of health failure while running a "routine" 10-mile jog. Jim Fixx was known in the running world as a prolific writer and marvelous personal motivator for other runners. He advocated running as a central component of a highly healthy lifestyle. His loss was felt deeply in the running community.

There were some who pointed to Jim Fixx's death as a morbid testimony to their supposition that one's health status is locked-up in one's genes, that one's genetic heritage blindly determines all physical eventualities. They were quick to claim that Jim Fixx's running did him no good. "Look at what happened to him," they asserted, "Dead at age 54!" Running, they argued, not only didn't help him, it actually may have hastened his death. They used his unfortunate death simply to buttress their own belief in a rather passive approach to health and wellness.

Actually, Jim Fixx was taking great self-health care responsibility. He was from a heart disease prone family. His father had died very young of heart failure and his brother had died at age 38 of the same ailment. Certainly these events, and the underlying meaning of them, served to motivate Jim Fixx to modify his lifestyle and adopt running as a means of dealing with his familial trait of early heart disease. Once the true facts of his family history were made more public, it became obvious that Jim Fixx had actually prolonged his life <u>and</u> had immeasurably enriched it along the way by incorporating running into his lifestyle.   Jim Fixx had taken positive self-health care responsibility; he exhibited a high degree of positive self-health care responsiveness.

Resources

Websites

WebMD > *Healthy Living* > *Healthy Seniors*
http://www.webmd.com/
Healthy seniors center – find information on senior health care, Medicare and aging related topics

AARP > *Health*
http://www.aarp.org/health/
Health and healthy living, exercise and wellness, Medicaid and drug benefits

Wellness.com
http://www.wellness.com/
Wellness & Health – Mind, Body, Spirit, Relationships

U.S. Dept. of Health & Human Services (HHS) > *Home* > *News*
http://www.healthfinder.gov/
Healthy Aging: The 60s – A New Beginning

Mayo Clinic
http://www.mayoclinic.com/
Medical information and tools for healthy living

Real Age
http://www.realage.com/
Information on looking younger and living longer

Section Three:
Finances & Insurance Arena

Introduction

Your **Finances and Insurance Arena** includes all that you have learned about finances in general and also a sense of how to manage your personal finances. Like most of us, you probably learned your fundamental attitudes about money and finance in your very early years and carried this wisdom (or this baggage) for a long time.

How well are your attitudes and information about money serving you today? Contrast how you think of money today, to how your parents thought of money, and how your siblings and your children (if you have any) think of money. Money plays a significant motivational role in our lives. Money can offer a sense of security when we feel our finances are in order, and a sense of foreboding if we feel they are not.

What Color is Your Retirement?

Here's a bit of financial wisdom I had offered to me by a Minneapolis cab driver when he heard I was headed to give a retirement seminar.

If your <u>outgo</u> exceeds your <u>income</u>, your <u>upkeep</u> will be your <u>downfall</u>.

"That's why I'm driving a cab at 70 years old," he said.

Not that there's anything wrong with driving a cab at age 70 years young, but if I did it, I would like it to be of my choice rather than forced by financial necessity. I guess most of us do what we have to do to "make ends meet." However, when we are coerced to do so by a lack of funds, this may push an otherwise smooth retirement into a serious detour.

The fact is that money is the first requirement for a successful retirement; without some level of financial support your retirement lifestyle will lack any real style at all. That's probably not what you have in mind for yourself and your loved ones. This of course is why we need to dedicate considerable time, energy, effort, and a portion of our income for most of our life preparing for this time of life called retirement.

This book is not a financial manual; it's a general overview of internal and external factors and forces, that contribute to living your retirement years well. However, since finances are so important (but not **all**-important) for retirement well-being, we needed to include here the salient aspects of money management that were common to all persons preparing for retirement, as well as those already in their retirement. When we considered the full scope of the truly necessary items on this list, we came up with three separate issues, each of which is covered on your <u>Life Options Profile</u>. These three are:

1. Knowledge of Financial Issues
2. Financial Planning
3. Financial Confidence

You'll find a separate chapter devoted to each of these three in this section.

What Color is Your Retirement?

Chapter Seven

Knowledge of Financial Issues

With increased knowledge and understanding of finances in general, you can rest a bit easier and with more certainty that your financial picture in retirement will remain stable. Having such a perspective is life-giving as you approach the retirement years.

So what information, which data, and what facts should you know as you tackle this financial "thing?" There's no foolproof answer to this question, and certainly this book can't possibly offer a comprehensive list of the panorama of information to which most financial planners have access. Yet, what we've compiled here is a basic list of terms and definitions that can constitute a fundamental foundation so you can get a firmer grip on your financial situation. Make the following words and concepts a part of your vocabulary and you will have taken the first step toward expanding your understanding of money management, savings, and investment.

Annuity Account: A tax deferred family of investment tools that are actually life insurance policies that pay you an amount of yearly income from the investment you made earlier. Annuities have become somewhat complex in that there are many variations of them. Annuities come in all shapes and sizes, however there are three major types of annuity accounts: **1) variable, 2) fixed, and 3) immediate**. A **variable annuity account** pays you a variable amount of yearly income that is based on a formula that includes your age, your expected mortality, the amount of money in your account, and the returns that account is generating. **A fixed annuity** pays you a predetermined amount of yearly income as previously specified by you. The amount of income you receive in a fixed annuity is based on the amount of money you funded in the account and mortality tables. **An immediate annuity** account begins paying you right away after you set-up (fund) the account. The amount of your yearly income from the annuity is determined, again by the amount you funded and mortality tables. An immediate annuity account can be set-up on a variable or a fixed annuity basis, or even a combination of the two.

Average Life Expectancy: The number of years that you can expect to live based on normal mortality tables at any given age. Many retirement financial planners prefer to use *maximum life expectancy* rather than average life expectancy. Maximum life expectancy is usually expressed as the percent possibility that you will live to a certain age. For example, at age 65 there is a 5% chance that you will live to be 100 years old, and incredibly a 1% chance that you will live to see your 105th birthday.

Bond Market Index: A bond is a financial obligation, or promise made by a company, government entity, or other organization. Bonds range from municipals to junk bond. Bond market index is simply the average change in value of all bonds in a particular class of bonds, during a period of time. This is usually calculated on a yearly basis. Investing in a bond market index fund means that you enjoy (or not) the gains or losses of the entire bond market.

Compound Interest: Literally earning interest on interest. For example, if you have a savings account that pays an annual rate of 5% interest, and you invest $1,000, after year one you would have $1,050. In year two you not only earn 5% of the $1,000, but you also earn 5% on the $50 interest you were paid after year one. Over time, your $1,000 grows dramatically due to the "magic" of compound interest: If you invested $1,000, here's what your original $1,000 would be worth after 20 years at the different interest levels indicated.

% Interest	1yr	20yr
5%	1,050	2,653.30
8%	1,080	4,660.96
10%	1,100	6,727.50

Disposable Income: The amount of money you have left to spend on "wants" after all your debts/obligations/bills are paid.

What Color is Your Retirement?

Diversification: Choosing a variety of investment vehicles rather than putting "all your eggs into one basket." When you diversify your holdings across different retirement investment vehicles, i.e., 401(K), Roth, Keogh, SEP-IRA, etc., and a variety of investment types, i.e., stocks, bonds, mutual funds, savings, annuities, etc., you minimize the risk you would otherwise take by using only one or two investment vehicles and investment types.

Guaranteed Benefits Pension: A plan for giving employees income in their retirement years, where the number of dollars the employee will receive each month in retirement is fixed. The amount of money is based on a formula (devised by the employer) that takes in account the salary of the employee (usually the average of the employee's highest five years salary) and the number of years the employee has worked for the employer.

High Dividend Stocks: Certain common or preferred stocks declare dividends each year. These dividends are separate from whatever capital appreciation (or depreciation) occurs with the stock price.   Some companies regularly declare annual dividends and so are sought by investors as a means of securing a stream of income.   Selected mutual funds are constructed exclusively of company stocks that regularly declare higher than the norm (whatever that is) dividends.   Such funds are called high dividend stock funds.

Investment Allocation: The practice of assigning certain pre-specified portions of a retirement nest egg to various investment types or vehicles.   For example, you might decide that 50% of your portfolio be placed in stock index funds, and 50% in bond index funds. You might allocate your nest egg assets 20% REITs, 25% bond index funds, 25% growth funds, and 30% money market funds. Your allocations will probably change over time as your level of risk tolerance changes. Allocation is like diversification, but a bit sharper in that it normally specifies a particular percentage of one's total nest egg be invested in certain types of investment vehicles.

Investment Risk Tolerance: Also called the "sleep well factor." Generally seen as the level of risk you can handle in your investments. An investment portfolio of 100% common stock would traditionally be seen as a high-risk tolerance allocation. Lower risk portfolios would be stock and bond index funds, large cap mutual funds, REITs, and certain select mutual funds consisting of Fortune 500 companies.

Market Timing: Trying to buy investments when prices are low and sell high. Keeping the pulse of the marketplace and attempting to "time" your investment sells and buys based on your own assumptions as to whether the market is going up or headed down.

Nest Egg: The total amount of money you have at your direct disposal to fund your retirement years the day you move away from full-time work. The notion of retirement nest egg is different from total net worth, which includes home equity, life insurance cash value, as well as other assets that are not specifically set aside for your retirement income purposes.

Post-Retirement Expenses: Your financial obligations in any given period of time (usually monthly or yearly) once you have entered retirement.

Portfolio Balancing: Reviewing your various investments to determine if any adjustments (investment types, risk tolerance, etc.) are needed. Usually done yearly.

Real Estate Investment Trust (REIT): An investment vehicle or "trust" that owns commercial real estate and passes nearly all of the rents along to shareholders. Dividends earned by REITs are generally a bit higher than other commercial paper because the real estate investments are leveraged, i.e., you buy more than the face value of your investment. This is the same leveraging principle as owning your home: you buy with money down and finance (mortgage) the remainder.

Replacement Ratio: The percentage amount of your pre-retirement income that you will need to sustain an equal lifestyle in your retirement. Generally we think in terms of a replacement ratio of 80%, i.e., needing 80% of your pre-retirement income to sustain you adequately in your retirement years. The wild card that dramatically impacts your required replacement ratio over time is the generally increasing simple inflation rate. As the inflation rate increases you will need successively higher replacement ratios to sustain your accustomed lifestyle.

Reverse Mortgage: The sale of your house to a lender with the provision that you can remain in your house and the lender (bank) pays you for your dwelling over time usually by sending you a monthly check. The term "reverse mortgage" comes from the payment action. Since you are no longer the homeowner, the lender (the new owner) pays you, the home dweller, rather than the conventional mortgage arrangement where the home dweller is also the homeowner and pays the lender a monthly installment on the mortgage. At the end of the day, subject to certain provisions, when you vacate the house (either by death or changing domiciles) the lender takes full possession of the dwelling and usually sells it at market value. Some retirees use reverse mortgages as a means of funding their living expenses.

Rollover: The term, rollover is generally used to describe moving your retirement funds from your company sponsored retirement plan to your own, individual IRA when you terminate your employment with that company or organization. Rollover is a legal procedure where a tax advantaged investment account is shifted from one brokerage firm to another firm. Rollovers can happen whenever the investor decides to do this, but most commonly happens when an employee moves from one employer to another employer. Also, upon retirement, the employee will generally "roll over" her/his account(s) to another privately solicited brokerage firm. If the account is not "rolled over" to some other brokerage, it may be 1) subject to ordinary tax provisions, and 2) the owner of the account is "fined" a 10% penalty for early withdrawal if she/he is under the age of 59 and one-half. Once this rollover procedure is applied, the account then carries the designation "rollover account" in addition to whatever other descriptors it may carry.

What Color is Your Retirement?

Safe Withdrawal Levels: How much money can you take from your retirement nest egg each year and for how long can you do this? Calculators have been devised that can tell you to the penny how much you can withdraw from your retirement nest egg. You "crank in" 1) the amount of your nest egg, 2) the number of years you need it to provide an income for you, and 3) the level of risk, or rate of return on the funds remaining in your nest egg after each withdrawal, and presto, the calculator will give you an amount of money you can "safely" withdraw from your nest egg each year (month) and have it last for the period of time you specify. Clever huh? One well-known calculator is the Portfolio Survival Simulator by Bill Swerbenski.

Savings: Simply stated, saving is putting a portion of your current income aside each year to build your retirement nest egg. While this is the most important retirement planning action, only about 60% of all Baby Boomers (persons born between 1946 and 1964) regularly save in a retirement tax advantaged saving plan.

Stock Market Index The average change in value of all stocks during a period of time. Usually calculated on a yearly basis. There have emerged many stock index mutual funds that invest in all stocks and therefore perfectly (or near so) reflect the entire stock market index. Investing in a stock market index fund means that you enjoy (or not) the gains or losses of the entire stock market.

Tax-Advantaged Savings Account: Any investment account where the federal and state (most of the time) taxes are deferred until a later date (usually at the time when you begin withdrawals) both on the original investment and the earnings from that investment. Examples of tax-advantaged savings accounts are: 401(k), 403(b), SEP-IRA, Keogh, Roth IRA, and annuities. All investments and earnings from these investments are deferred from taxes until you begin withdrawing it at which time it is taxed as regular earned income. The Roth IRA plan is different, you do pay taxes on what you put in the Roth but you do not pay taxes upon withdrawal. In all plans you cannot begin withdrawals (there are exceptions) until you reach 59 and one-half years of age, and you must begin taking withdrawals at age 70 and one-half years of age.

Naturally, these few investment concepts are only a small part of the increasingly complex field of investment management. You always want to obtain the best advice and information from a professional financial planning specialist.

What Color is Your Retirement?

Chapter Eight

Financial Planning

You will greatly improve your chances of achieving your goals when you have a plan. This principle applies to many, if not all life situations, but it seems even more obvious when we talk financial preparedness for retirement; unless of course you are independently wealthy, in which case we would say that you are even more in need of a comprehensive plan, since you have much more to lose if you don't.

To make a truly workable financial plan, we recommend that you connect with a partner to help you. This partner is normally a certified financial planner, a person who has the knowledge, skills, and specialized competencies required to construct a comprehensive plan, shoulder-to-shoulder with you. A higher level of financial planning tends to minimize uncertainties by giving you a course of action that is "in place" for the many eventualities and possibilities that can fly your way in retirement. Financial planning covers some rather simple things like having a will, having proper insurance policies in force, and knowing where, how, and in what proportions your retirement nest egg is invested.

Perhaps the best retirement financial plan is one that is started early in life and is adhered to over the long haul. So many times we debate the benefits of one financial strategy or tactic versus another. Certainly there are better financial plans than others, no doubt, and the merits of one can be debated over the merits of another ad infinatum. Yet, it's the virtue of self-discipline, in sticking to the plan that you've adopted that is more important than the relative advantages of one plan over others. So, the best financial plan is one that starts early and stays the course over the long haul ... self-discipline and steadfastness.

There are more financial planning strategies out there than politicians have exceptions; yet, there are commonalities among the majority of them that are worth considering here.

The Best Savings Strategies: All retirement financial plans start with saving. Exercising the self-discipline to begin saving so early in your life that it almost seems irrational to do so ... is a wise move. It's probably impossible to start saving for retirement too early in life. One woman's ideas on saving gave me pause when she said that *saving is over-rated*. I had the distinct impression when I heard this that she would one day be sorry she ever thought like that. Saving is necessary, necessary, and necessary! Now if you are approaching retirement and realize that without knowing it you had subscribed at some level to this woman's savings philosophy, you are struck with the realization that you do still have some possibilities: 1) win the lottery (not likely), 2) rob a bank (not recommended), 3) come up with some pretty creative financial strategies (perhaps), 4) keep working for a paycheck, at least at some level (more likely), or 5) allow the State to care for you (welfare, Medicaid, or jail) ... can you think of any others? Save in any way that you can, if you're lucky enough to work for an employer who matches your tax advantaged accounts (at any level) this is the best savings of all.

Life Insurance: Life insurance has a place in your overall retirement financial planning picture.   This is especially true when you are younger; it's also a good idea in your later years, for perhaps different reasons.   For one thing, life insurance (whole life policies, or whole life-like policies here) is a form of imposed savings self-discipline.   While the rate of return on life insurance premiums is not the highest rate you could achieve, the nice thing about it is that you are paying those premiums like clock work.   There may even come a time when you actually forget that you're paying the premiums; you don't miss the money you're putting away for your retirement, because that's what a good life insurance policy can turn out to be for you.   Life insurance is considered the foundation of any financial plan.

A Budget: It might seem strange, or even elementary to consider a budget as part of your financial planning schema but it should not be overlooked. The earlier you establish a budget and commit yourself the better your financial picture will look over time.   A budget is an elementary financial planning devise that enables you to allocate your income into places where you want it to go so that you don't get over-exposed in any one area, or over-extended into others.

Conspicuous Consumption and/or its cousin Competitive Acquisition: Here are the two most venomous retirement financial planning vipers. Basically, living beyond your means. Conspicuous consumption is buying things just for the sake of purchasing them, only because you *want* them ... not because you have any true *need* for them. Competitive acquisition is often about keeping up appearances just for the sake of looking good. Competitive acquisition is an extension of the retort you used to give your mother when you wanted something ... *"Well, Johnny has one!"* Try to recognize when and how you might be caught in this, and then vow to get yourself out of it. Do you really need that new car, or do you simply think it would look good for all the neighbors and friends to see you driving down the street, or into the church parking lot in it? Simplify your life, learn to enjoy trips to the library rather than trips to the casino, perhaps a trip to the next state might be just as enjoyable as a two week cruise. Learn to change your thinking about the purpose of money.

Human Capital: Are you as good to your body, taking good and kind care of it, as you care for your money? Are you good to your mind, not overloading your thinking and feelings with unnecessary and unkind thoughts and emotions? What about your intellectual assets? Do you intentionally exercise your brain, stimulate your mind, and invest in its improvement? Do you take classes, go for another degree, and fill your mind with the noblest thoughts? And what about your soul, your spiritual life? Do you find peace and harmony, purpose and meaning, joy and compassion in your life? Can you address the larger questions in life: Who am I? Where am I going? What gives you a sense of awe, wonder, and delight? These are spiritual questions and they offer a solace that enables you to better enjoy what ever financial resources you have accumulated. Investments like these play a role larger than you may think in your overall financial planning.

Relocation: When we think of relocating our residence in retirement we generally think about moving to a warmer climate, a more hospitable geography, etc. Yet relocation can serve more than one master. Some relocation in retirement is about simplifying your life, about downsizing real estate assets, about slimming your outgo for house and home. Now, if you can move to a more preferred geography and at the same time put your monthly rent or mortgage on a good diet I guess we could say that you have "double dipped." You have achieved two goals at the same time. The point here is that relocation can be part of your retirement financial plan just as much as your 401(k) is. Lowering your total housing cost by four or five hundred dollars, or whatever relocation brings you in lower housing costs, is the same amount you raise your disposable income.

Working: If you've read the section in this book on working after retirement then you know that many retirees also work. You can work for the joy of it, because you're improving the world, you're giving something back. But, if you can work because you really love the work AND get a paycheck too, well then, that's all the better! The fact is that many retirees do work, and some even work because they need the money.

Many retirees start a business. This can be a good idea in lots
of ways, but cutting into your retirement nest egg to fund it
must be very carefully considered.

A Four-Legged Stool

Typically we think that most people's retirement will be
funded from four sources: **1) federal social security payments,
2) employer's pension plans, and 3) your own personal
savings, 4) compensation from working.**

.

Social security is over-extended and the imbalance will
only tip more each year.   This means that the federal
government will be forced to do two things: a) cut benefits,
and, b) lower payouts; realistically it will probably do both.
Social security will survive, but at what levels it will survive is
anyone's guess.   Chances are that the level of support from
social security that you previously expected probably won't be
there ... it will probably be lower.

Today, only 16% of retirees receive guaranteed-
benefits pensions from their employers; that means that 84% of
American retirees do not! That's the good news; the bad news
is that the fiscal health of many guaranteed benefits plans is in
jeopardy. The federal government has established the Pension
Benefit Guaranty Corporation to "guarantee" worker's pension
benefits for retired workers from those private companies
whose retirement benefits plans have failed due to bankruptcy.
This government guarantee fund is now also over-extended; at
the time of this writing Congress is trying to plug what could
become a mammoth drain on the federal budget if more and

more corporations bail out of their guaranteed worker's benefits plans and "dump" their responsibility onto the federal government.

The third leg is your savings, the only truly reliable source of retirement funding. Responsibility for funding your retirement is squarely on your own shoulders, and that's where it's liable to stay for a long time. The bad news here is that most baby boomers are off to a slow start. Nationally, retirement savings rates are way below the levels that would truly guarantee adequate retirement funding.

The fourth leg of course is any earned income you can generate from your own post-retirement work.

Conclusion

Whatever your financial condition, it's recommended that you consult a professional, a person you can trust, who can made a realistic assessment of "where you are" financially, and can help you construct a plan that can work for you.

What Color is Your Retirement?

Chapter Nine

Financial Confidence

Confidence is a measure of internal security and surety that a particular task can, in fact, be accomplished. Confidence is seen in the retirement preparation situation as the premier emotional ingredient contributing to the eventual success or failure of the undertaking.

To what degree do you feel secure that your retirement financial plan will sustain you and your family for your entire retirement stage of life? Confidence is a mixture of: 1) an understanding of the task at hand, 2) the evaluation that one's capabilities are sufficient to achieve success in the undertaking, and 3) the felt sense, or feeling that you can succeed. Lack of any of these three would lead to avoidance of the task at hand.

Confidence cannot exist on its own, we must have confidence in something; confidence must be attached or associated with some basis in fact, or some perception of reality. We need to feel that our decisions are sound and will produce results that will bring us a financial security that we hope for. Confidence cannot be the result of wishes, but rather of resolutions that are backed up by solid actions intended to accomplish prescribed actions leading to desired outcomes.

If you look up "confidence" in your handy Thesaurus, you'll find words like: assurance, certainty, positiveness, spirit, boldness, self-reliance, communication, faith, trust, and courage. Well, I guess you need all of these to be truly confident in your retirement financial plan, but who is totally confident? I once met a man who was genuinely scared that he didn't have a big enough retirement nest egg; turns out that he had six million dollars! Some time after that I was talking to another man about his retirement security; he told me that he was *"all set,"* his retirement nest egg was all of $55,000. *"How much more would I ever need?"* he said.

Both of these men were living in an illusionary blindedness about retirement; neither had bothered to conscientiously consult a certified financial planner who had a specialty in retirement issues. Neither guy had done his retirement "homework" and consequently hadn't a clue about their real financial needs for retirement. The guy with the six million dollars was living a delusion, and so was our $55K friend. Neither was genuinely confident. How could they be? They didn't have all the facts.

Confidence is a relative thing because confidence is essentially a feeling, a felt sense. All your feelings, however, are based on your thoughts. And where do your thoughts come from? To answer that question we might need a little psychology lesson.

Your personality is totally unique to you; no one else has an identical personality to yours, yet there are commonalities. Your personality operates through six functions; 1) believing, 2) perceiving, 3) thinking, 4) feeling, 5) deciding, and 6) acting. You generally move through these six in sequence at lightening speed, even though you're only rarely aware of it. So, when we apply this framework to your financial confidence, we can see that confidence is in the fourth, or feeling function. Confidence is created by the thoughts you put in your mind, that come from your perceptions (data you take in). Your perceptions emerge from your beliefs, attitudes, and values about whatever you're focusing on.

Let's apply this framework to our two friends mentioned earlier because one has no confidence and the other has distorted, or false confidence. Below is a comparison of their beliefs, perceptions, thoughts, feelings, decisions, and actions.

What Color is Your Retirement?

Function	$6M Man	$55K Man
Beliefs	Retirement goes on Retirement is expensive	Retirement is short
Perceptions	Family has struggled With retirement	Same job/steady pay no family struggles
Thoughts	Full of questions	Someone else will take care of it
Feelings	Trepidation; no confidence	Blissful ignorance; false confidence
Decisions	No logical decision	No logical decision
Actions	Over action	Little or no action

The $6M man probably believes that retirement stretches on forever and that it's dramatically expensive. He also has a related and confounding question among his beliefs, that if you're not working, do you even deserve to receive an income? The $55K man probably believes that retirement funding is a snap, that $55K is a grand amount of money, that he can live off the "fat" of the land (or off someone else ... like the government), and that retirement is a relatively short time anyway. He probably doesn't even believe that he'll ever spend the $55K! The point is that neither man confidently knows!

Our two friends perceptions of retirement are also quite different. The $6M man has seen some of his own friends and family financially struggle in retirement. He had to financially help his father for the 15 years before his death. The $55K man always worked for the same company (with no guaranteed pension plan), always got a steady paycheck, always had a spouse that also worked, and never saw any of his friends or family struggle in retirement. Here we see two very different perceptions, or experiences about retirement.

When it come to their thinking function, the $6M man is full of questions, while our $55K man doesn't ever lose a wink of sleep about money; he lives by the adage, *Don't worry, someone else will take care of it*. So what feelings do you think each of our friends has about retirement finances? The $6M man is filled with trepidation, while our $55K man is blissfully, but blindly secure. Each man remains unaware of his distorted position.

As a consequence neither man can make logical decisions about their finances, and therefore takes no action. Both men are stuck in their delusions. You might say, *Well, that's true but the $6M man will fare all right*. Would you call worrying everyday of your retirement faring well? Certainly not! The whole point of financial planning is so you won't be worrying every day about finances, isn't it? Our $55K man is the one in for a rude surprise; he's probably headed for a financially woeful retirement existence called welfare. This is not our idea of a happy ending.

Conclusion

True confidence is the central power behind your motivation to live a full and satisfying retirement lifestyle filled with whatever "tasks" you choose to pursue. Without it, you flounder in a sea of uncertainty that causes you to live below the life satisfaction level and "tasks" that you'd otherwise pursue.

What is that "task" in your retirement years? If you spent some time in section one of this manual, you probably have a good idea what that particular retirement task(s) might be for you. The general task we all seek in retirement is multi-faceted: finding peace and purpose, interest and stimulation, play and rest, care and compassion, justice and fair play. Most of us want all these things, and more from our retirement years, and you can get them, but you need confidence. Confidence is not an option; it's mandatory for a successful retirement.

Resources

CNNMoney.com > *Personal Finance* > *Retirement*
http://money.cnn.com/retirement/index.html

The Motley Fool > *Retirement*
http://www.fool.com/
Retirement Center

AARP > *Money and Work* > *Financial Planning and Retirement*
http://www.aarp.org/money/financial_planning/
Financial Planning and Retirement – Pension, Estate Planning

SmartMoney.com > *Retirement*
http://www.smartmoney.com/retirement/

U.S. Social Security Administration
http://www.ssa.gov/

About Retirement Planning
http://retireplan.about.com/
IRAs, Roths, 401k, mutual funds, stocks, bonds, wills

NewRetirement.com
http://www.newretirement.com/
A retirement calculator, information and services for creating a viable retirement

Kiplinger's Personal Finance > *Your Money* > *Retirement*
http://www.kiplinger.com/personalfinance/money/retirement/index.html
Investing for retirement - your guide to making money work

What Color is Your Retirement?

Section Four:
Family and Relationships Arena

Introduction

Every list I've ever seen about the characteristics that make for strong mental health includes the ability to make and keep friends, the ability to develop, nurture, and maintain intimate relationships. Yet, why is relationship building so important? Why are we so compelled to interact with one another?

On a physical level we have a long heritage of developing relationships. In our primitive state, mankind depended upon cooperation with his and her companions for survival. An individual person was decidedly vulnerable on the open range or forest. When humans learned to cooperate through communal hunting, defense, gathering food, and the like, their chances for survival rose significantly.

Such cooperation allowed humans to form tribes and/or communities. In a very real sense, the better the tribe became at relationship building, the greater their chances for ultimate success, expanded property, wealth development, and power. Relationship building now went beyond survival and included socialization and cultural development.

On a psychological level, we learn who we are through our relationships. It is in encounters with others that we come to better understand what is actually on our minds. We are constantly in search of growth, of individuality, of becoming all that we can become. The better we can express what we are thinking and feeling, the more accurately we can come to know the uniqueness of this wonderful personality that has been given to us.

On the spiritual level, relationship building is the story of our ongoing dialogue with a higher power. In a very real sense we come in contact with the divine as a consequence of our interactions with others. As we deepen our relationships with others we quite naturally grow closer and closer to the core of our personality, the place where we find the divine within. Here is where we discover spiritual intimacy, that condition where we come to know and to share our most closely held truth, beauty, and goodness.

We Need Relationships

We crave relationships. When we engage others, even on the most superficial levels, we actually feel better, we feel belonging, greater security, greater safety. Abraham Maslow, the renowned psychologist gave us a hierarchy of personal needs; he claimed that we organize our lives to satisfy these five broad areas of need. They are:

1. Physical needs: food, clothing, shelter
2. Safety and security needs: protection from threat
3. Belonging needs: the need to be part of a group
4. Self-esteem needs: the need to experience the affirmation of others
5. Self-actualization needs: the process of becoming all we can be.

Relationship building fosters the satisfaction of all five levels of human needs. No wonder we are compelled to form relationships; without them we would fail to thrive.

What Color is Your Retirement?

Chapter Ten

Flexibility

Flexibility is your ability to change. How and why is it that some adults in retirement revel in change: they embrace it with gusto and glee? These 'high' changers seem to capture all that is new, they are vitally interested in the world, they relate with others freely, they find stimulating endeavors that delight their souls. In short, they are fully alive and totally healthy. Yet, we find other retired individuals who seem quite the opposite. They resist change of any kind; they seem to want the world as it was yesterday. They may show their reluctance through irritability, depression, withdrawal, and avoidance, even denial.

Alvin Toffler's book <u>Future Shock</u> appeared way back in 1970 and has since been regarded as a milestone. The book made the forceful case that our culture is moving so fast that those who have not mastered the skills of change will suffer. He called this condition of change resistance, "future shock."

He wrote,

> "...it became clear that future shock is no longer a distantly potential danger, but a real sickness from which increasingly large numbers already suffer. This psycho-biological condition can be described in medical and psychiatric terms. It is the disease of change." (page 2)

Toffler identifies retired adults as most vulnerable to future shock because their formative years were in a time when the pace of change was much slower than today. Consequently, they were not forced to learn the skills of change and have not been able to pace themselves to the tremendous "..roaring current of change, a current so powerful today that it overturns institutions, shifts our values and shrivels our roots." A new retirement mentality can change this rather dismal prediction.

Remember your earliest memory; what was occurring? You have a memory of this event because something changed within you, some belief; in some dramatic way you came to some startling realization on that occasion. Why else would it remain imprinted in your memory after these many years if you somehow hadn't changed in some way at that particular time? Your life shifted then, in some way you changed; you added to a belief, shifted your perception, injected new thoughts into your life, experienced very stimulating feelings, made a life shifting decision, or took robust action. In some significant way, you changed your life, or your life was changed for you on that fateful day. On that day, you matured.

Adult development and maturation is about change! When you were a baby, and for the first time you got up off your all-fours and took your first steps, on that day you matured. When you went off to school, on that day you matured. When you had your first date; when you took your first job; when you left your family of origin, over and over, and on and on you matured. Maturation is good; it is part of the master plan.

You can't escape maturation; certainly you wouldn't want to, you would miss all the "stuff" of life. Yet somehow, when the maturation process proceeds into the middle and later stages of living, we want to squirm out of maturation, at the very least we want to slow it down. We start digging our figurative heels into the dirt of the present day and begin refusing the future, refusing the developmental imperative. On that day we start turning our backs on change. When that happens, we close down to growth, we start to die and we repress what could be a meaningful retirement.

Flexibility works to our advantage spiritually, providing that we remain open to change versus trying to hold onto the thinking and feelings of our previous years. Change means that we shed some of what was before and replace it with internal growth. As we mature we are supposed to increase in wisdom, in charity, in faith, in hope, in trust even though at times we are forced to become more dependent. As our body may experience diminishments, our true, spiritual self experiences growth like never before.

What Color is Your Retirement?

Flexibility affects our lives at every level; it allows growthful change. This change occurs physically, mentally, emotionally, psychologically, and spiritually. Our fear of change, this so-called resistance to change, can be seen so easily in others yet we can seem quite blinded at times to the need for change in ourselves. *"If she would only take care of herself a bit more she would be so much more appealing!" "If he wasn't so grumpy all the time I would talk to him more." "Why doesn't she _____ more?" (fill in the blank)* Statements like these and many others so strikingly point up the ease and clarity of our perception when viewing others. If we could only be so observant and casual about spying our own shortcomings!

So often it's not until we are pushed to the proverbial edge that we reluctantly make the behavior changes that perhaps could have been made more efficiently some time before. How many smokers didn't quit until their doctors had already discovered health damages from smoking? Or how many retirees now wish they had saved more earlier? How many divorces could have been avoided if one or both partners had been able to move to forgiveness sooner, or away from criticism earlier? Indeed, why is it that marriage counselors are doing a booming business while marriage enrichment seminars are notoriously sparse in attendance?

Most people don't change until they are pushed by compelling challenges that would exact some kind of pain if changes were not made. Even though change is the natural order of things, change is certainly not revered as the premier agent of growth that it is. As Douglas Smith wrote in his book

Taking Charge of Change (Addison-Wesley, 1996) "*Threatening circumstances and challenges compel both performance and change much more effectively than mere opportunities and good intentions.*" (page 6)

We find it difficult to recognize change as the overall wellness and happiness enhancer it is for retirement. We tend to ignore or deny change rather than embrace change as our friend for growth and development. Every day is supposed to bring something new. Every day then is about change. Yet, do we regularly seek changes that would improve our health and personal development? Do we undertake the "work" necessary so we can develop a mindset that stimulates change in us? We need to be ever open to the possibilities of changing.

Take Risks

One of the competencies that grows from openness to change and flexibility is the ability to take risks. No, not a devil-may-care attraction to impulsivity or carelessness, but a measured, considered ability to make choices that generally involve uncertainty. Without risk taking we would find ourselves safe and secure, but perhaps lacking in personal luster, spark and a sense of accomplishment. The retiree who doesn't join the local fitness club, on the pretext that he must save his money; the retiree who prefers the security of his home TV to a stage show or theater venue; the retiree who passes-up new developmental classes, citing disinterest in the subject; all these and many more like them, may trace their lack of motivation to an inability for taking a risk...fear of the unknown. "Taking the plunge," "going for it," putting oneself "on the line," all speak to the same quality...to shouldering some form of risk. One's risk taking ability can mean the difference between a retirement life of monotony and one of personal growth and internal accomplishment.

Permission to Fail

No one wants to fail, yet failure is an essential part of life. We seek to avoid failure, yet to what lengths will we go, how much energy will we devote to the cause of failure avoidance? Sports psychologists tell us that the best performance in the athletic field comes from adopting a mental attitude of *"play for the fun of it."* Why do we seem to adopt a mental attitude of *"play to avoid losing?"* One attitude gives permission to "fail" (lose) as an inevitable part of playing. The real "failure" here is failing to have fun. The other attitude places winning, or "failing to lose" as the highest good. Personal satisfaction, here comes from avoidance rather than achievement....a very passive and non-spirited way to play the game. So too, retirement can be seen as a game. How would you like to play it...'avoid losing', or 'for the fun of it?'

Uncertainty is the number one cause of stress in our lives, and yet the opposite, not enough change, can paradoxically, also create stress. It is the latter, not enough change, not enough stimulation, that causes stress in the lives of many retired adults. Some retirees find themselves falling into what has been called the "cow path" mode of living. This is when today is lived out very much like yesterday, we don't allow change to enter into our lives. We may become fearful of change, fearful of what tomorrow may bring to such a degree that we figuratively walk the same course that we did yesterday, psychologically playing the game that *"if it worked yesterday, it's sure to work today."* The trouble with living a "cow path" lifestyle is that sooner rather than later we begin experiencing stress reactions. We can become irritable, bored, depressed, lethargic, unresponsive, self-absorbed, and simply out-of-sorts. Refusal to change guarantees that you'll change in ways that you probably won't like.

Tolerance for Ambiguity

One of the surest ways of deadening your life in retirement is to demand consistency...trying to control events, circumstances, and even other people, trying to conform them into your own notions of what or how they should be. Without realizing it, we can descend into a rigidity of thought that pushes us to direct our "world" in ways that we want. When we demand, we stifle our patient inner guide, we denounce the fairness of flexibility and contort our view of reality into a confined complexity that breeds internal turmoil. All of this can reduce a lifestyle, retired or not, to a rote repetition of the same behaviors, the same discussions, the same thoughts and guarded feelings, or we can enrich living to a robust quest for fullness and uniqueness.

Change requires that you learn how to place trust in yourself. With all the adjustments and all the modifications that are asked of us as we mature, it's common that some self-doubt invades our psychological space from time to time.

What Color is Your Retirement?

Change is hard because it always demands that we forfeit something, that we lose something. Loss may be the driving force behind positive, constructive change. At every life stage we must face losses, and as a consequence of these losses we are compelled to change. When our last child leaves home to strike out on his or her own, we experience loss; when sickness strikes, we experience loss; when we see our parents die, we experience loss; when our first grandchild is born, we experience loss (we lose the status of being only a parent), this list expands as we mature. Each of these losses mandate change; the change can be external as in the case of sickness where we lose the ability to go to work or play, or it may be internal where we are forced to shift our attitudes about being the oldest generation when our parents die. These changes are sustaining, they allow life to go on and growth to continue. Without change life soon dies.

Any and all personal successes begin with change. Success doesn't come from staying the same; it requires change. Think of a success that you have experienced, a public success like buying a new home, or a private success like giving up smoking, losing weight, or learning to get along with someone who had formerly been disruptive to you. Any of these successes requires change and usually requires loss.

Flexibility breeds openness to change, and change awareness breeds personal growth and development....your retirement stage requires all three....flexibility, change, and growth.

Chapter Eleven

Caregiving: Aging Parents

Certainly we are called to care about, and sometimes to care for our aging parents. Because of this, we're all called to learn healthy caregiving methods and attitudes if we are to live the successful retirement that we'd like. Whereas everyone and certainly every family is different, there are some common threads that weave through all successful caregiving.

Never before have we been called to the degree, nor to the duration of caregiving that we seem to be today. No matter what walk of life we happen to find ourselves, married or single, a majority of us will be called to the caregiving role in one way or another. All projections of national population shifts predict mammoth changes in the relative and absolute increases of senior persons in our culture. Centenarians are the fastest growing group of persons in our country today; those 85 years of age and older are not far behind. All these changes are to the good.

What Color is Your Retirement?

The medical community is working overtime to keep our bodies functioning and alive ... and it is succeeding. Every new medical advancement, every new miracle drug, and every new enhanced rehabilitation procedure increases the number of medical survivors, and thus increases need for caregiving. Whether these newly conscripted caregivers are adult children of their own aging parents, or spouses who have been thrust into prolonged caregiving roles for their own wives or husbands, the ranks of caregivers swells everyday. It increases enlistment in this army of caregivers who, with little or no basic training, are drafted into service that may require all their strength, and all their faith for a duration that only God knows.

Those of us who are called to caregiving, and chances are we will all be at some time in our lives, are also called to make choices ... many choices. Naturally, many of these choices involve decisions on the material level: food preparation, schedules, time and assets management, and so forth. Yet, perhaps the most far-reaching decision we will be called to make is in how we are to conceive of the caregiving responsibilities we are called to shoulder!

The Strain of Caregiving

Investigations into what has come to be called the "strain of caregiving" have surfaced the fact that it's not the physical burdens of caregiving, nor even the financial strains that cause the most turmoil and difficulties for caregivers; surprisingly, it's the emotional strain. It's the flood of feelings that constantly swirl around the caregiver and sometimes threaten to drown them that cause the most confounding confusion in their lives.

Some time ago I conducted a study that found that adult children caregivers had many positive feelings toward their aging parents but they also reported experiencing an equal level and intensity of negative feelings at the same time. On the one hand they reported feeling such positive emotions as: love, concern, caring behavior, protectiveness, sympathy, respect, empathy, compassion, gratitude, admiration, and responsibility; while on the other hand, at the same time, they also reported such negative feelings as: anger, frustration, resentment, annoyance, pity, impatience, aggravation, guilt, sadness, distaste, and helplessness.

Such a split in their feelings presents an emotionally confusing paradox for caregivers. Feeling two distinctly different, even opposing sets of feelings at the same time can cause waves of inner turmoil for caregivers. One especially demoralized caregiver once said to me: *"I feel like I'm circling the drain."* Her image was one of being caught in the vortex of swirling water just before it disappears down the bathtub drain. I found her words painfully descriptive.

Some caregivers experience no strain at all while others seem to be continuously "circling the drain." Many factors, some personal and some familial, contribute to the depth of strain any individual caregiver will encounter. There are, however, some themes of caregiving that can help.

Gems of Caregiving

Studies and investigations into the caregiving role, whether the caregiver is an adult child or a spouse, have unearthed some gems of caregiving. One of these gems is that there seem to be nine potential steps that can actually elevate the caregiving role into something personally enriching for the caregiver. I've seen these stages of growth and development operate in many different guises, yet the general momentum of the steps seems to be universal.

1. Feeling sorry: When sickness or disability strikes someone we love, it's almost automatic to feel sorry that his or her life has been physically diminished. Caregivers can become overcome with thoughts of "*Isn't this too bad! This shouldn't have happened to him/her, she/he is such a good person.*"

2. Heroic acts of caregiving: In sympathy for the losses experienced by the loved one, caregivers can, in the emotion of the moment, commit to caregiving levels that they are really not able to sustain over the long haul. They want to bring things back to "normal," bring them to their best conclusion; they want to "fix" the situation and may eagerly accept responsibilities that are really beyond their capabilities.

3. Confusion: When their best efforts don't seem to be having an impact on the situation, caregivers can move into an emotional turmoil where they seem to question everything: their capabilities, their intentions, their commitment to their

loved one. Self-depreciation and self-discounting are the consequences of this confusion.

4. Anger and resentment: While caregivers do not universally feel anger and resentment, some feel them acutely. *"Why is this happening to me?" "Why did this have to happen to me at all?" "I need to get out of here."* Thoughts like these and many others can invade the once clear thinking of the caregiver and render them depleted in spirit and drained of energy.

5. Depression: When step four remains unresolved, depression of some sort becomes almost inevitable. Caregivers feel stuck, helpless, hopeless, and unable to focus on any other issues in their life. Fun and leisure become out of the question. All energies, however meager they have become, are so narrowly focused on the loved one that caregivers can lose themselves in the process.

6. Information seeking: Caregivers move beyond depressive feelings by reaching out for assistance. There is always some form of help out there in the community: support groups, faith sharing groups, counselors, community services, church support, hospital offerings, etc. are all geared to help those who need it.

7. Empathic identification with other caregivers: Even if the caregiver can find one other caregiver with whom they can share their experiences, that's usually sufficient to unburden themselves emotionally just enough so they can restore some of their spirit and personal energy back.

8. Forgiveness of self: How necessary is this stage? I've seen caregivers berate themselves for what they think they should be doing, they think they ought to be doing, or even for what they are thinking and feeling. Moving toward self-forgiveness can remedy this unfortunate guilt that so often emerges in the face of the caregiving process.

9. Letting go: *"Let go and let God"* is the adage that makes so much sense here. It is only through an active and creative acceptance that caregivers can emerge from the strain of care to find themselves refreshed and rejuvenated.

Needs of Caregivers

The very first need of caregivers is <u>information</u>. Caregivers require information so they can give the best care possible without endangering their own health, well-being, and growth. This information falls into six categories.

1. Develop an understanding of their loved ones' needs, as well as their own needs. This understanding includes a deep sensitivity to emotional needs as well as the more easily recognized physical needs.

2. Learn to develop and strengthen truly healthy relationships with the one for whom they care. Such a relationship is the fundamental element of caregiving. It includes the three conditions of any quality relationship, namely: genuineness, warmth, and unconditional positive regard.

96

3. Learn how to break down barriers that may exist between themselves and the one cared for. Examining attitudes about aging and older persons in general is useful for the caregiver, as well as recognizing how myths about aging may be playing a role in one's caregiving.

4. Foster positive communication between themselves and the one cared for. Caregivers can learn active listening and psychological attending skills; listening to the meaning behind their words and offering empathetic feedback. Communicating empathy requires skills to reflect content and feelings.

5. Sharing love helps caregivers maintain a positive and meaningful attitude. Knowing factors that contribute to "successful aging" and incorporating the notions of life stages and transitions into one's thinking are useful for both caregiver and the one cared for.

6. Come to a better understanding that the final end of caregiving is not "fixing" but rather the end of mortal life. Knowing the five stages associated with death: denial, anger, bargaining, depression, and acceptance helps caregivers deal with death and grief.

These six broad areas of knowledge make up the core of what caregivers need to know in order to deal comprehensively and confidently with their caregiving roles in faith, hope, and harmony.

What Color is Your Retirement?

Chapter Twelve

Caregiving: Adult Children

Your children are dear to you and you always want them to be happy. Some parents seem to give of themselves too little, while others give too much. When parents "over-give" to their children they can negatively affect their children's growth and development as adults. Such children may remain dependent, and ultimately become angry with the very parents who tried so hard to help them.

Our society seems to delay the 'breaking away from the nest' process more and more. Since 1970 there has been a 34% increase of 18-24 year olds and a 150% increase of 25-34 year olds living at home with their parents. There are many reasons for these increases:

- In general, starting salaries are not keeping pace with the cost of living and housing costs have risen dramatically.

99

- People are delaying their marriages. In 1950 the average marrying age for women was 20, and 22 for men. By 1990 these rose to 24 and 26 respectively. By 2005 average marrying ages continue to rise, settling in at 26 for women and 28 for men.

- Divorce of both parents and their adult children has sometimes forced them back into living together. Changes in parenting, allowing freer access to the old homestead is another factor.

- Adult children who decide to move back to live with parents often do so as a result of a loss or crisis: loss of job, unexpected expenses, retreat from personal pressures, or a relationship break-up.

- Additional or advanced study can also cause a move back home, as can other changes in lifestyle.

Once adult children do come back/or postpone leaving home, the initial concern and care from parents can easily grow into resentment and sometimes into self-recrimination, i.e., blaming yourself for your child's situation.

Pressure on parents seems to be increased in cases where the adult child moves back home (also called the re-filled nest) versus having never moved out in the first place. When adult children return home, parent's life satisfaction can decrease, while stress and conflict can increase. Both parents and adult children require some effort so they can adjust and accommodate to the new living arrangement.

Finances

An important retirement factor is the financial impact of returning adult children, also called *Kippers* (Kids in Parents Pockets Eroding Retirement Savings). Kippers is a slang term referring to the predicament of parents whose adult children are out of school and in their working years, but still dependent upon their parents. According to recent studies, most parents report that having Kippers can be a pleasant experience. However, it usually results in the parents saving less than they otherwise would for their retirement.

Because economics is such a powerful motivator, more adult children return home when economic times are tougher. Census figures show that 56% of men and 43% of women ages 18-24 today live with one or both parents. Some never left, while an estimated 65% of recent college graduates have moved back in with their parents. ("Returning to the Nest" The Baltimore Sun Feb. 29, 2004).

New York Life, a leading financial planning company says it plainly on its website
www.newyorklife.com/cda/0,3254,13762,00
"The return to the nest can become a financial burden that can derail the parents' plans and jeopardize their financial future, especially their retirement, as they try to do too much for their children." New York Life offers "how to make it work," that advises:

1. Set house rules

2. Set a departure date
3. Insist on responsibilities
4. Help adult children restructure debts
5. Do not sacrifice your own financial future

Psychologist and TV personality, Dr. Phil weighs in with his own advice for parents facing live-in adult children on his website: www.drphil.com/articles/article/138

- Set boundaries without feeling guilt
- Let your adult children plan their own lives
- Think about the true meaning of help
- Prepare your children for the world

Dr. Phil goes on to give advice for the adult children living at home:

- Take responsibility for yourself
- Have a plan to get out on your own

The 'Never Empty Nest'

Beyond the 'empty nest' filling up again, we often now have the *never empty nest* a situation where children never have left home. The children have 'earned' several new names: "fledglings," "incompletely launched," or "near adult." Here are some recommendations for this situation:

Recommendations for Caring Parents of Adult Children

1. It's best to let your child know what you expect

2. Make clear conditions that affect your comfort with regard to: music, visitors, neatness, hours, etc.

3. Offer encouragement, not advice. Most adult children know they should be out on their own and would rather be

4. Respect your adult child's right to privacy

5. Listen to each other

6. Set a timetable for departure

Whether the living situation is the "never empty nest," or "re-filled nest," some clear understandings need to be worked out. According to Child and Youth Health website: www.cyh.com, parents with adult children living with them need to decide such things as:

- How much board or rent is reasonable?
- Who will shop for groceries?
- Who will do the cooking and other household chores?
- Are parents willing to lend their car and under what circumstances?
- What rules are there for the adult child's visitors?
- Who will pay the phone and/or the Internet and TV cable bill?
- What are the conditions for respecting each other's privacy, noise level, etc.?

What Color is Your Retirement?

Sandwich Generation

The *Baby Boomers* (those born between 1946 and 1964) have been the most studied generation in our history. As a group, Boomers are thought of as being somewhat self-centered ... the so-called "me" generation. Yet Boomers seems to invest more of themselves and their resources into caregiving than even previous generations. Because of several social factors including greater longevity, later marriages (which mean that adult children generally live at home longer) and higher financial needs to start a household of one's own, Boomers have had to "step up to the plate" and provide care not only for adult children, but simultaneously to aging parents as well. The term "sandwich generation" has been used to describe this "in the middle" position that Boomers occupy between their adult children and their aging parents.

An AARP (American Association of Retired Persons) study of Boomers in the sandwich generation situation, found that many appear squeezed, but not overwhelmed by the sandwich issue. Seventy-four percent say that they are able to handle their family responsibilities, and most say that they do not feel overly stressed by family issues. However, the ones who feel the stress of the sandwich issue feel it severely. Three in ten Boomers site significant stress arising from their care and support of older and younger generations. Lower income families site higher levels of stress. Interestingly, 69% of all respondents in this study of Boomers rejected the idea that their own children should be expected to take care of them in their old age.

Family and Relationships Arena

In a study by the Pew Research Center, some interesting caregiving statistics emerge on the sandwich generation. Consider these numbers:

- 68% of Boomers help their adult children financially
- 29% of Boomers help their parents financially
- 13% of Boomers help both their adult children and their parents financially
- 66% of boomers feel parental responsibility for children's college bills
- 33% provide housing for adult children
- 56% provide housing for elder parents

Radio talk show host Dennis Prager www.worldnewsdaily.com brings up another point to ponder. Some adult children, both those who never left home, or those who turn into *boomerang kids* (once out but have now returned) may find living with parents just too comfortable. He says, *"Far more adult children stay home today because it is often quite pleasant to live with one's parents. ...This generation of adult children was raised with more freedom, autonomy and respect than probably any in history ...a vast number of parents make their homes far more livable, even enjoyable for their children than parents in the past did."* He points out that it's not the fact that adult children are living with their parents, but what are they doing with their lives when they're living with their parents? If adult children are clearly working hard to improve or advance their lives, then living at home is much more pleasant for all since a clear goal for eventual independence is in place. On the other hand if adult children spend their days watching TV and partying all night, then living at home has turned their parents into enablers of unhealthy and non-productive behavior.

Conclusion

Close to 14 million adult children are still living at home with their parents. Living at home can be productive and profitable for the adult child, and even enjoyable for the parents, but like anything else, guidelines need to be formulated and agreed upon by all concerned if the situation will result in a gradual growthful path toward eventual healthy independence for the adult child, or whether shock waves of conflict rumble through the adult child/parent relationship, especially when those parents are either already retired, or preparing for it.

Chapter 13

Grandparenting

Grandparenting is an opportunity to play, to "fall in love" again, and to appreciate the magic of a new person developing. Grandparenting allows us to experience the world in a new way, through the eyes of a younger person. It's an invitation to learn about what's on the minds and in the hearts of today's young people. The grandparent/grandchild relationship is like no other. It needs to be nourished with warmth and guidance that can only come from a grandparent. And when it is, the grandchild can feel free with grandparents, can feel appreciated and loved in different ways than even their parents can give.

The Ohio State University website has perhaps the best information on grandparenting around. www.ohioline.osu.edu Here's a taste of it ...

Approximately 75% of Americans over the age of 65 have grandchildren, and most begin the role in their middle years. The average age of becoming a grandparent is 51; there are some societal forces that are bringing this down (teen pregnancy) and others that are forcing it up (later marriages), so the average age seems to be fairly stable.

The early grandparenting years are generally very busy ones. Early grandparents are very active people; many are employed and may be involved in caring for their own parents as well as their grandchildren. In addition, early grandparents are involved in their own life changes and transitions that add stress to this time of life. But grandparenting for most people is not seen as a stressful time, unless the grandparent takes on a hands-on caregiving role with their grandchildren.

There are lots of benefits of grandparenting, among these are:

- Being involved in your grandchildren's lives
- Providing family support and encouragement
- Learning with experience
- Legacy building

Recommendations on Being a "Good" Grandparent

- Listen to your grandchildren
- Talk to them, but don't lecture
- Love your grandchildren for what they are
- Baby-sit only when it fits your schedule
- Don't take on parental roles
- Avoid complaining to your grandchildren
- Be enthusiastic and encouraging
- Laugh a lot

- Have fun with your grandchildren
- Take time to just "be with" your grandchildren
- One-on-one is sometimes better for everyone
- Build a relationship, every step counts

Distance Grandparenting

Sometimes called 'remote grandparenting' or 'tele-grandparenting,' grandparenting when your grandchildren are not living close by can be a challenge. Our geographic distance from one another is one of our societal realities. But distance in our modern world doesn't mean estrangement. Long distance grandparenting presents some special challenges, but the goal is the same, establishing a close relationship. Exchange emails frequently. They don't have to be long; it's the thought that counts. Send things along to your grandchildren: books, CDs, pictures – these things are appreciated more than you know. Visit when you can, and invite your grandchildren to come visit you too. Remember, grandparenting is primarily developing relationships that last for life.

The Internet can add a whole new dimension to distance grandparenting. In addition to frequent emails, instant messaging, and setting up 'chat-dates,' grandparents and their grandchildren can share websites of mutual interest. As the grandchild grows and their interests change, there are always new websites to explore, new ideas to investigate, and new relationships heights to shoot for. Video conference calls add still another opportunity for keeping close.

What Color is Your Retirement?

Another good website for grandparenting is the American Academy of Child & Adolescent Psychiatry: www.aacap.org. As you might imagine, the main thrust of this site is good mental health. Here are some of the points they make.

Grandparents as Parents

Grandparents are an important resource for grandchildren; they provide childcare, financial assistance, and emotional support. Increasingly, grandparents are forced to take over the primary caregiver role for grandchildren when parents are not present. When grandparents take over this primary "parental" role they serve as parents and do more than just nurture and reward their grandchildren. They must learn to set limits and establish controls as they did with their own children. These are tasks that non-custodial grandparents should not take over when parents are present.

Many grandparents in this care-taking role underestimate (or are unaware of) the added burdens their new role as 'parents' will place on them. Sometimes this new role, coming at a time when grandparents may be ready to simplify and slow down a bit, can evoke feelings of anger, loss, resentment, and even guilt.

Custodial grandparents need support and information. One good place for information is the AARP website: www.aarp.org. Another website that provides quality information is:

www.helpline.org/life/grandparenting

Family and Relationships Arena

Here you'll find lots of information. Here's a taste:

Establishing some ground rules with your adult son and/or daughter is a good first step to ensure that potential problems and pitfalls don't emerge. What role do your grandchildren's parents want you to perform? What are they comfortable with, and what are they not? Grandparents need to be ever respectful of the desires and decisions of the parents. Listen closely to your grandchildren, make notes about their interests, pet's names, books they've been reading, TV shows they like, doll's names, anything you can repeat in the next conversation so that they know you are really listening and interested in them.

One wonderful function of grandparents is to pass on the history of the family. Share pictures and tell stories about their parents and about yourself that give your grandchildren a sense of belonging and uniqueness. Try to be as specific as possible not only in the descriptions you give of people, things, and events in your early life, but perhaps just as important, try to share how you felt when you were going through the same years as they are now.

Be as active with your grandchildren as you can; get out and go. Simple things like hikes through the woods, resting by a pond, noticing a bird, and teaching them a song along the way are all great activities for children, and especially so with grandparents. See sights, play games, take a trip, share your interests, talk about work, and communicate about family history.

What Color is Your Retirement?

<u>Step-Grandparenting</u>

Blended families --- when two previously married partners each with their own children get married --- are on the increase, consequently, so are blended grandparenting families. Step-grandparenting can present awkward moments and add a level of complexity to the grandparenting role, especially when other grandchildren are already in the picture. It's estimated that a full one-third of all retired persons are step-grandparents and the numbers are growing. A blended family calls for heightened levels of compassion, interest, understanding and of course ... patience! In general, new step-grandparents need to go slow, give time for whatever mourning needs to be accomplished, time to let all family members, both old and new, learn about one another and find good common ground.

Conclusion

The advancing role of grandparenting is expectantly anticipated by parents as they watch their children take that incredible step into parenthood themselves. It seems everything changes when adult children become parents themselves; in very real terms the same is true for the new grandparents. Grandparenting is grand, it's supposed to be. Grandparenting is that natural progression into a new role and a new stage of living. The benefits of grandparenting are expansive, some are enumerated above, but most are beyond the scope of words alone ... grandparenting is simply one of those things that must be experienced to be fully appreciated.

Resources

Flexibility

Prepare your Marriage for Retirement
http://www.msnbc.msn.com/id/7187691/
Advice from Dr. Stephen Treat Director and CEO of the
Council for Relationships

Men are from Mars, Women are from Venus
http://www.marsvenus.com/
Relationship advice from 'Men are from Mars, Women are
from Venus'

Caregiving

AARP > *Family, Home and Legal* > *Caregiving*
http://www.aarp.org/families/caregiving/

Family Caregiver Alliance
http://www.caregiver.org/
Information, education, services, research and advocacy for
caregivers

The AgeNet Eldercare Network
http://www.caregivers.com/

Helpguide > *Aging Issues* > *Caregiver Support*
http://www.helpguide.org/elder/caregiver_support.htm

Books

Johnson, Richard P., Caring for Aging Parents,
Concordia Publishing House, 1995
Johnson, Richard P., How to Honor Your Aging Parents,
Liguori Publications, 1999

Grandparenting

AARP > *Family, Home and Legal* > *Grandparenting*
http://www.aarp.org/families/grandparents/

Grandparenting.org
http://www.grandparenting.org/
The Foundation for Grandparenting

Helpguide > *Active Healthy Lifestyles* > *Staying Connected* >
Grandparenting
http://www.helpguide.org/life/grandparenting.htm
Expert, non-commercial information on mental health, healthy
lifestyles and aging

Grandparents Today
http://www.grandparentstoday.com/

Section Five:
Leisure and Social Arena

Introduction

Your **Leisure and Social Arena** is an ever-broadening and dynamic arena for those who have 'graduated' from their full-time work role. All that you like to do when you don't have to do anything else is contained in your leisure arena. Fun and play, hobbies and sports, relaxation and rest, and so much more, are all parts of the leisure arena. In your retirement years, however you conceive of them now, you will most likely spend much more life energy in your leisure arena than you did in your full-time working years.

You'll find four parts to the Leisure and Social Arena covered in your Life Options Profile. These four are further described here: Chapter 14) Your Leisure Preferences, Chapter 15) Retirement Residence, Chapter 16) Travel, and Chapter 17) Hobbies.

What Color is Your Retirement?

Chapter Fourteen

Your Leisure Preferences

Having fun means that we can devise, pursue, and even master our own psychology of leisure. Leisure requires our active motivation, planning, organizing, and follow-through; it requires our proactive energies. Leisure is a manifestation of our inner selves ... a part of our own personal psychology, our own personality.

Leisure can be defined as the degree to which you have found personally satisfying endeavors outside or inside your work that can rejuvenate your body, stimulate your mind, and/or enrich your spirit. All leisure is not created equal. One person's leisure is another's work. Some leisure activities sound anything but leisurely. Hang-gliding, bungee jumping, autocross racing, or even snow boarding are all great releases for some but to others such activities sound only a heartbeat away from torture. Likewise, volunteering in a homeless shelter, delivering absentee ballots, cleaning "trashed" streams, or picketing for peace and justice issues can all be marvelously enriching and stimulating to some people, while others would categorize such activities as tedious at best or simply boring. What then makes leisure, leisure?

First, let's look at the different categories of leisure. All leisure activities are generally seen as fitting into six categories:

1) *Social Interaction*: Activities where you engage in an interpersonal exchange of ideas of a satisfying nature. Activities ranging from simple, casual conversations, to active and well-planned affairs such as galas, dances, parties, and social "get-togethers." Other activities that are almost entirely "social" would include having a cup of coffee with a friend, sharing a secret, a "win," a personal triumph or a loss.

2) *Spectator Appreciation*: Activities where you watch others participate in any kind of activity. "People watching," sports events, concerts, parades, theater, opera, dance and many other spectator engagements qualify for this leisure category.

3) *Creative Expression*: Any activity that "taps into" your unique creativity. This would include all artistic endeavors, but also everyday kinds of things as well, such as: how you cook your eggs, how you care for your car, how you mow the lawn, how you talk, walk, dress, and even how you

pray. Creative expression includes all that you do that bears the indelible mark of your own personal creativity.

4) *Intellectual Stimulation:* Activities that enhance your mind. These would include anything from reading, studying computer manuals, "surfing" the net, watching educational TV programs, attending a lecture, intently following current events, a stimulating conversation, cross-word puzzles, listening to self-help CDs; the possibilities are endless.

5) *Physical Exercise*: Any and all activities that cause you to move your body parts. This can be organized and purposeful activity like a round of golf or a game of tennis, or walking the local mall, working-out at the gym, training for a marathon, cycling cross town, paddling a kayak, even flying a kite. In addition, this category of leisure would include physical activity associated with your everyday activities as long as you were mindful of the leisure quality inherent in the activity.

6) *Solitary Relaxation*: Activities done alone, from just sitting and rocking, to bird-watching, jogging, a solo walk, knitting by yourself, to a relaxing bath. Being alone can be quiet, leisurely, and profoundly relaxing, rejuvenating, enriching, and rewarding.

Leisure: A Fundamental Human Need

Leisure is a human need, without it we eventually get sick. Some of us need generous amounts of leisure while others of us need only a relative fraction, but all of us need leisure to some personally satisfying degree. If we work hard enough, long enough without a break, without a respite, and without the soothing balm of leisure, we <u>will</u> get sick. Leisure is a need!

When we have no leisure, we risk a gradual erosion of our genuine human spirit.   Leisure relieves the built-up pressure caused by our use, and sometimes overuse, of our physical and mental faculties. Leisure unwinds those thousands of rubber band-like life strands that can become tightly coiled and even knotted as a result of prolonged mental and/or physical exertion. Leisure offers us respite in a world that otherwise demands too much.

Leisure and Stress

Leisure has several paradoxes; it operates seemingly the opposite from the way our common sense would expect. For example, when we are stressed we seem to require more leisure as a respite than other less stressful times in our lives. We are all well aware that stress can come from being overloaded with things to do and pressures from the press of a harried pace. Yet, few people realize that stress can also come from living a lifestyle that is <u>under</u>-loaded. Studies have shown that prolonged inactivity can give rise to stress in our lives just as easily as over-activity can. Under-stimulation in our lives, under-utilization of our gifts, talents, and personal resources can be a source of stress for us and require that we remedy such an imbalance in our lives with leisure.

Leisure usually commands a more central position in our retirement years. Before retirement we saw our work as the central cohesive factor in our lives, yet in our retirement years, leisure receives more of our life energy than it had received throughout our work lives, perhaps more than it had received since our childhood. Yet leisure in our retirement years is different in manner, style, and intensity than we had witnessed during our full-time working years.

Leisure...Valuable Human Endeavor

While some individuals will consume their lives with leisure activities, other maturing adults, fail to see that leisure is a valuable human endeavor at all. Either extreme is unhealthy. We all need to recognize our personal leisure needs and act on them if we hope to achieve maximal health and wellness in our retirement years. When we depreciate our leisure needs we discount our own sense of self. When we depreciate our leisure needs, we lose sight of our true nature and risk falling prey to the attitude that we live to work; that our worth rests in our work alone. Such an attitude can derail the direction and momentum of any retirement.

What Color is Your Retirement?

Leisure reminds us that our sole purpose in life is not simply to do, but to be. When we recognize fully that we are first and foremost a human being; when we gradually come to appreciate our essential self, we can begin to move away from a definition of ourselves as an achievement/production machine, and move closer toward a more balanced, and accurate definition of self. As we transform ourselves away from work as the chief definer of our life, we can come to see our leisure interests and pursuits as part of our life journey. In this sense, leisure helps build in us a sense of wholeness, because we grow to realize that our inner nature is the cohesive and binding force in our lives; that force which gives integrity to our world and balance to our lives.

Leisure is more than simply performing activities that please us. Leisure includes a contemplative mode of internal perception. This internal leisure allows us to rediscover our child-like qualities of awe, and wonder, and delight. This special leisure refreshes the spirit, and is a wellspring of rejuvenation. When we rediscover these child-like ways, we can better see the beauty that surrounds us. Marie Therese Ruthmann said, "The celebration of things as they are is the soul of leisure."

Life without leisure renders you spiritually anemic. Leisure bears gifts in abundance; meaningful gifts that you would probably not receive from any other source. Leisure bears gifts such as: motivation, creativity, exercise, entertainment, relaxation, self-confidence, and socialization. And when we escalate leisure to its higher level, we see that these leisure gifts become even more generous, providing

122

meaningful roles, offering opportunities for making important contributions, transforming lifestyles, and creating the capacity to serve others.

When the challenge of leisure is not resolved in our maturing years, we face some dismal consequences. We find it almost impossible to reflect on the true meaning of living. Our life degenerates into a shallow routinized mechanism for doing things and performing tasks. We find it difficult to truly appreciate the beauty and the loveliness of the present moment. We can become callous and anxious, self-centered, and self-absorbed when we fail to meet our leisure needs. Developing a leisure attitude gives us the pause to be grateful, and in the process, leisure grants serenity.

What Color is Your Retirement?

Chapter Fifteen

Residence

Where shall I live in retirement? The question raises a cascade of additional questions that get to the very heart of what's truly important about retirement living for you. Should I construct a new lifestyle in a new setting? Should I "retire in place" and continue to enjoy my familiar surroundings? Can I keep up friendships from a distance? Can I move away from the grandkids? Should I move closer to the grandkids? Questions like these, and many more, make the retirement residence issue a pivotal one. Let's try to sort it out.

Want to Move?

For those who want to move to a new retirement residence, take heart because the options are almost endless. Luckily or not, finding information about your retirement residence of choice and preference is second only to financial planning in the amount of data and advice that you can glean right over the Internet. There are few life decisions as personal as where you live and the type of abode you prefer; it's like finding the right glove. There is an ever-expanding panorama of options of retirement living in our increasingly retirement-savvy culture. One needs only to enter "retirement living" in your favorite search engine and *presto* you are inundated with more information than you'd ever thought possible. So how do you begin to sort it out?

There are a number of factors that you need to consider right from the get-go so you can begin to focus your search. Questions like the following, that were taken from the www.bestretirementspots.com website may help.

1) What kind of climate do you like? Do you like humidity or do you prefer a drier climate? How does elevation affect you? What about temperature?

2) How important is it for you to be near family? Is a central location in relative close proximity to your family a priority for you?

3) Do you like participating in social clubs, community groups, athletic oriented groups, religious organizations, and the like? Is it hard for you to join new groups, or is this a strength for you?

4) How important is proximity to top-notch health facilities? Does your health insurance cover you in your proposed new retirement residence?

5) Are you a lover of the water? The ocean? The mountains? Open spaces? The desert? Have you ever lived in any of these or are they just dreams of yours?

6) Do you like change? Are you good at meeting new people, trying on new lifestyles, modifying your schedule?

7) Will you volunteer in your new community? Does it have sufficient opportunities for meeting new people and engaging in new activities? Is it "retirement friendly?"

8) Do you like lots of activity or are you looking for a place to "kick back?" Do you like nightlife, athletics, the outdoors ... does your proposed retirement residence offer any of these?

9) Is accessibility to an airport important? How important is travel for you, and can you satisfy your travel plans from your new site?

10) How important are educational opportunities for you?

11) Can you afford to live in this proposed location in the style to which you've become accustomed?

What Color is Your Retirement?

These questions should help you dig deeper into yourself. They should also serve as discussion starters for you to entertain the ideas of the person (people) you love. You might even want to write your responses to these questions; they will undoubtedly motivate other questions that are ever more personally relevant for you.

Are You the Retirement Community Type?

Retirement communities are a virtual growth industry in our culture, they seem to be popping-up everywhere. Certainly the traditional retirement states like Florida and Arizona offer a vast array of possibilities at almost every price level, but more and more retirement communities are by no means confined to the so-called retirement states.

College and University Towns offer a bright retirement living alternative. The first college retirement communities opened about 20 years ago, but the idea has really spread of late. There are at least 50 retirement developments around the country and that number should double fairly soon. Graduates from that college or university are the first to sign-up, but increasingly, retirees are finding that the cultural, sports, and educational opportunities offered by living around a campus are hard to beat. The projects vary widely, some are condominium developments, frequently with community centers, others are continuing care centers, while most are single family homes nestled close, but not adjacent to the college or university. The appeal of living near an educational institution is clear, and the active lifestyle modeled by the college kids can be enticing and youth preserving.

128

High-Rise Urban living has a different appeal. High-rise retirement buildings in busy downtowns are not the norm, but the idea is coming around. The lure of all that activity, entertainment, cultural affairs, shopping, educational proximity, good public transportation, and immense diversity and variety are all "pulls" that certain types of retirees find irresistible. And of course, urban living doesn't require you live in a specified "retirement building," the residential options are as varied as the people who live in a major urban area. Lofts are "big" especially in the older cities. Some loft projects report that up to 25% of their unit sales are to retirees, who either want a part-time city residence, or a permanent full-time residence.

Country living offers a peaceful atmosphere at a cost that is almost always less than the cost of living in-town, in destination resorts, or golf communities. Country living, whether it be in a formal retirement community, or in your own residence generally provides a caring, convenient environment that meets personal needs. The country is much more than a housing development, instead it's a community where programs, activities, and services are locally based and generally handled with a charm that may be missing in other places. Traffic and parking are not considerations, taxes are usually low, and perhaps most importantly, in a small town or rural area, people generally get to know you better.

Planned Retirement Communities seem to be sprouting up everywhere. Variety is the word in planned retirement communities; you can expect to find a wide variety of living styles, an even wider variety of home, condo, co-op, or apartment styles, and certainly a huge variety of prices. Many are so-called "continuing care" residences, which means a mix of 1) active living homes, apartments, or patio homes, 2) independent living where some services are provided, 3) assisted living where more personal services are offered, and 4) skilled care living where full medical and personal care services are required.

Other planned retirement communities are for active maturing adults only. These are the ones that appeal to some recently retired folks. Here the accent is on activities, activities, and more activities. The lifestyle is punctuated by a variety of activities that seems endless. Whatever might strike your fancy is offered in such communities. Here's a description of one such community: *"Surrounded by meandering walking trails and calming ponds, the centerpiece of the community is the magnificent 12,000 square foot community clubhouse and recreation center with indoor and outdoor swimming pools, fitness center, tennis and sport courts, a putting green, billiards, ballroom, card room, and craft room."* (www.retirementliving.com/RLnewcomm.html) This description is "mild" as compared to others that become ever more inclusive and even opulent.

Resort destination retirement communities have always been popular and are becoming even more so. Resort destinations, or at least resort areas continue to draw the largest numbers of relocating retirees. But the resorts are expanding. The Missouri Ozarks region, for example has exploded as a retirement settlement site, the North Carolina mountains, the

Las Vegas surrounding towns, the Texas Hill Country, and the Pacific Northwest have all enjoyed dramatic increases as retirement residences. Naturally the ocean is a perennial draw; indeed, water of all kinds, lakes, waterways, and rivers, it seems even ponds attract retirees in droves. Mountains are a close second; the Rockies, the Appalachians, the Ozarks, all attract numbers of retirees. Of course there are some well-heeled retirees who spend one season near the water and another in the mountains. Indeed, split residence is perhaps the fastest growing style of residential living for retirees who can afford such pleasures. Historical "resort" destinations such as Williamsburg, Virginia or Gettysburg, Pennsylvania attract their share of retirees. "Fun" destinations, such as Las Vegas, Disney World, Myrtle Beach, North Carolina, Hilton Head, South Carolina, Cape Cod, the Maine coast (any coast). Educational and recreational destinations such as National Parks, (think Yellowstone and others), Interesting geological sites (think Royal Gorge, Colorado) and ecological sites (think Sedona, Arizona) all have their own special attraction to that unique retiree.

And of course we find **golf communities** specially targeted for retirees. Golf is so big that in some retiree's minds that even the word *retirement* starts and ends with golf. Golf is the gold standard of the retirement mentality in our culture. On a recent Google search using "retirement residences in golf communities" a total of 4,770,000 sites came up. There seems no shortage of retirement golf communities, but they keep going up. Retirees like the proximity of the golf game; they also like the clubhouse lifestyle where many social endeavors that revolve around the golfing lifestyle call to many as the ideal life of retirement leisure.

Conclusion

It's certainly an understatement to say that where to live in retirement is a very big decision. Desired residence is perhaps second only to finances as the number one discussed retirement factor. *"Where should we spend our leisure years?"* is a question that is asked and re-asked. Try to open up the discussion to its widest potentials and then begin narrowing your focus to include what's truly important to you and of course, what you think you can afford. One nice thing about residences ... you can always move!

Chapter Sixteen

Travel

People who like travel generally like change; they like new things, changing environments. Travel can provide a new perspective, a new way of looking not only at the world, but also at oneself. Your travel score on your LifeOptions Profile gives you an indication of how highly you value travel.

According to a well-respected global study on retirement trends called Retirement Scope, American retirees travel more than their counterparts in other surveyed nations. Interestingly, retirement travel is not as prevalent as pre-retirees might anticipate. While nearly 60 percent of today's workers expect to travel frequently, only about 31 percent of current retirees value travel as much. If these numbers hold up, we can expect today's Baby Boomer retirees to travel almost twice as much as today's retirees.

The Value of Travel ... Personal Growth

Travel is much more than getting from one place to another, more than driving to visit the grandkids. Travel has much more to do with enjoyment, retreating from the norm, and about personal growth. Travel, especially the type of travel that retirement living can offer, is best when it's a personal experience, a time to have fun, a time for deepening relationships, and a time for experiencing new things. All summed up, travel offers an invigorating means of becoming more who you really are, to live life more passionately, and to get in better touch with our authentic selves.

Personal growth is the natural change that occurs as we have new experiences and our beliefs are challenged. We can grow emotionally, intellectually, and spiritually over our entire lifespan, and travel offers a perfect way to achieve all of this. Every experience we have either reinforces what we believe or challenges us to reconsider our beliefs and attitudes ... the basis of our personality.

Travel causes us to delve deeper into ourselves and view ourselves, and the world, from a broader perspective. Travel can change our thinking, it holds up new data for us to consider, evaluate, and eventually fold into ourselves. Travel showers us with new feelings that inspire us, challenge us, motivate us, and most of all simply affirm us as unique individuals thoroughly involved in the flow of the world that is so much bigger than us.

Yet, almost paradoxically, travel allows us to value our uniqueness in expanded ways; at the same time, travel shows us how small we are, and yet how special and strong we are. Travel shows you a larger horizon, gives you a bigger canvas to paint your life masterpiece, it enriches your soul, and brightens your point of view. Because travel can do all of this, it allows you to consider new life options that may not have formerly crossed your mind.

Travel not only gives you an expanded outlook, it also gives keener insight so you can consider life more comprehensively, plan new endeavors, and capture new life objectives. Opportunities of all sorts emerge, internal potentials can become more concrete actuals for deeper personal growth, the possibilities of "you" can morph, with travel, into personal realities. Travel somehow can give us permission to follow that dream that may have only been an illusion in the past. Travel holds up for us a new freedom of action; old interior barriers can fall, releasing our authentic selves with confidence.

The Lure of Travel ... Wanderlust

Webster defines the word *wanderlust* as: *"A strong and unconquerable longing for, or impulse towards wandering."* Webster defines wandering as, *"Movement away from the usual, proper, normal course or place."* Some retirees seem to capture new life as they give in to their inner desire to go and see new things, and meet new people. They may have been bored with a life they regarded as too normal, too usual, too proper ... they want to break free ... they want to express

135

themselves more fully, they want to discover new spaces in themselves as they discover new places on the map, and delight in new faces along the way.

Travel ... the Expense

Travel can be invigorating, however, travel can be expensive ... it can be, but it doesn't have to be. Travel is like automobiles, they come in all shapes, sizes, and prices, but they all do the same thing ... get you from place to place.

Consider these travel options and try to rank order them in terms of cost from the most expense to the least. You might also want to rate each of these in terms of your own personal preference. In any event, check-out some websites under each of these travel categories, there you'll find tons of information, and in the process maybe even give yourself a romping case of wanderlust.

Cruises

Adventure Camps

Tours

Inner Awareness Programs

RV Travel

Backpacking

Leisure and Social Arena

Bicycling

Camping

Hostels

Monasteries & Retreat Centers

Kayaking

Beach Vacations

Lake Vacations

Service and Volunteer Travel

Educational Tours

Ecotouring

Exotic Resorts

What Color is Your Retirement?

Chapter Seventeen

Hobbies

Hobbies can provide a good deal of life-enrichment in retirement. Hobbies invigorate one's mind and heart, stimulate one's sense of inspiration and awe, and simply provide a creative outlet for something inside that yearns to come out. Hobbies also give a sense of accomplishment while offering opportunities for social interaction.

Your work in the leisure section of this book (above) can give you some good global ideas about what categories of hobbies you might find most satisfying.

Hobbies can provide lots of benefits for you, among them are:

- A sense of awe, wonder, and delight
- Motivation
- Creativity
- Exercise

- Entertainment
- Relaxation
- Self-confidence
- Socialization
- Meaningful roles
- Opportunities for making important contributions
- Potential to transform your lifestyle
- Capacity for serving others

Hobbies ... Always a Diversion

Hobbies are advantageous because they give us pause from the central cause of our life. In our full-time working years, the central life cause for most folks was to earn a living, and/or support a family, even if that family was a unit of only one or two. Hobbies allow us to rebalance our lives that can become "off-kilter." Any activity can become a hobby, but one retiree's hobby is another's work. In order for an activity to be a hobby it must fulfill two criteria:

1) Be physically rejuvenating, mentally stimulating, and/or spiritually enriching
2) Be a diversion from one's normal work

We can sometimes forget this second criterion: a hobby cannot truly be a hobby unless it is separate from work, and a diversion from work.

During your active working years, your work-dominated years, the balance between work and hobbies was tilted toward work. You expended much more energy at your work than at your hobbies. In your maturing years, and especially your retirement years, for most of us this balance reverses. Generally we spend much less energy on work related issues and more on leisure and hobbies. Nonetheless, it would prove counter-productive for any retiree to devote their full-time energies to hobbies because your life would not be balanced. Your hobbies would cease to be diversionary, and would therefore cease to be true hobbies.

This diversionary quality of hobbies can create a snag for retirees. First, retirees may have no work. Second, many retirees may believe that the purpose of retirement is for living a life completely full of diversions, leisure, and hobbies. How can one live a leisure lifestyle without hobbies? This appears to be a grand contradiction in terms. Indeed, here is the paradox: we cannot have true hobbies at all without first discovering our central life purpose, other than our hobbies. Hobbies must always take a secondary position in our life, there must always be some type of work, or what we could call "life cause" activities in a person's life for them to fully appreciate, enjoy, and gain from their hobbies pursuits.

When hobbies become your full-time endeavor, then your hobby becomes your work; it ceases to be your hobby. When this happens, the power of the hobby to provide rejuvenation, stimulation and enrichment is lost. The paradox of hobbies is that in order to enjoy hobbies you must have some type of work in your life, some type of activity from which hobbies can be a diversion.

What Color is Your Retirement?

Hobbies lose their luster when they take the full time center stage position in your life. Like a vacation spot loses some of its luster when you make it your permanent home because it is no longer an escape or a diversion from your everyday world. So too, the same hobbies that formerly gave pleasure cease to provide the same refreshment, stimulation, and enrichment when hobbies becomes your full time pursuit.

You may wonder how some retirees can play golf every day, or go fishing every day, or simply rest every day, or do any hobby every day and still gain pleasure and satisfaction from it. The truth is that they have simply replaced one job for another, one action for another. The same beliefs, attitudes, and values that drove them at work, continues to drive them at their new "work." Even though they appear to have shifted their lives dramatically, moving from full time work to full time golf, all they really have done is to shift from one activity to another. They may need to augment their lives with greater meaning and purpose by adding their personal life cause, their new work, to the mix of activities in their life. As the old saying goes, "All work and no play makes Jack (and Jill) dull boys (and girls)." So too, all play and no work can do the same. Hobbies help us balance our retirement lifestyle, and serve as a personal mirror reflecting back important information about ourselves.

Resources

Residence

CNNMoney > *Best Places to Retire*
http://money.cnn.com/best/bpretire/

Where to Retire Magazine online
http://www.wheretoretire.com/

Lifestyle advisor – by Del Webb
http://advisor.delwebb.com/advisor/
Serves as an invaluable tool to help map out a lifestyle that's perfect for you

Travel

AARP > Travel
http://www.aarp.org/travel/
Travel – destinations, discounts, transportation tips and lodging

Lonely Planet
http://www.lonelyplanet.com/
The world's best guidebooks, travel advice and information

iExplore
http://www.iexplore.com/
Adventure travel & world travel

National Geographic Traveler Magazine online
http://www.nationalgeographic.com/traveler/

Hobby

Find me a Hobby
http://www.findmeahobby.com/
Looking for hobby ideas? Hundreds to choose from with tip to get started

What Color is Your Retirement?

Retirement With a Purpose > Hobbies
http://www.retirementwithapurpose.com/hobbies/

Leisure Activities Finder (LAF)
A booklet listing over 700 leisure activities that match Holland Codes. (see Chapter One)   Available from Psychological Assessment Resources, Inc. www.parinc.com

Section Six:
Personal Development Arena

Introduction

Your **Personal Development Arena** includes all the active and intentional actions you perform that improve yourself. These can include personal reading, informal and formal education, self-discipline and self-vitality, practicing care, compassion, courage, kindness, patience, wholeness, independence, forbearance, authenticity, and many other civic and personal virtues. At its core, personal development entails becoming all that you can become, expressing your gifts, talents, and abilities as fully as possible.

The retirement years, of course, are times when personal development takes on more, not less meaning. In your retirement years responsibility for personal development shifts away from factors and forces outside yourself and rests more on your own shoulders. Your need for personal development doesn't lessen as you approach your retirement transition; in fact, it probably increases. Personal development in the past centered on how to keep your edge as a worker, a professional, a craftsman, etc.; today's central focus is more about how to keep your edge as a person. Your need for personal development hasn't diminished because of retirement, it's simply changed its primary target.

This section covers three broad areas of personal development. Chapter 18 introduces you to the essential need of life meaning. Chapter 19 looks at education in retirement while Chapter 20 talks about volunteering in retirement.

Chapter Eighteen

Life Meaning

Meaning is a felt sense; we experience or feel meaning. Meaning provides us with a sense that our lives are "on target," that we are somehow living a life that is good, true, and even beautiful. Meaning gives us the emotional sensation that we are "in sync" with ourselves, that we are balanced and authentic, that what we believe at our very core is actually being lived out in our lives; in short, meaning allows us to feel real.

Personal meaning gives us the expansive sense that we are part of a larger whole; that we are connected to a bigger order that gives us that wonderful security and stability of belonging, we are attached to something sure, something good. The opposite of this is alienation. Personal meaning advances our spirituality in that we are able to connect with something bigger than ourselves; we are "in touch" with goodness at some level. Personal meaning allows us to feel part of an overall plan; it stimulates hope and generates charity. Personal meaning allows us to fix our vision on that which is pure and

147

stable, and changeless: the love in us and all around us. When we discover our personal purpose we keep our eye on the transcendent goal of life; we can better shoulder the ambiguities of living on this planet.

Some retirees unfortunately experience the opposite of meaning; they feel a gnawing sense of emptiness and meaninglessness. It feels like there is something missing, like their "real" life is over, existing only in memories. Such an emotional floundering represents a significant health risk. The sense of spirit and life that was formerly there seems to have evaporated, or at least eroded. In such a state their vulnerability for sickness increases as their zest for life diminishes.

When all of this happens, depression is soon to follow. Depression is the number one psycho-spiritual malady of the senior years. In large measure this unfortunate situation is due to a lack of something worthwhile to live for. Yet it's not in major depression that we find the majority of retirees. Lack of life meaning is far more commonly expressed in retirees by a sense of frustration, worthlessness, and internal angst; all of which squeezes our lives and overshadows our spirit.

Survival for What?

Viktor Frankl perhaps said it best in his famous book Man's Search for Meaning, (Beacon Press, Boston, 1959) "The truth is that as the struggle for survival has subsided, the question has emerged: survival for what?" Ever more people today have the means to live but no meaning to live for. There is something much more to life than simply existing. At every

148

stage of our lives we need to be engaged in some challenging endeavor if we are to achieve "total health." Yet this endeavor is different for everyone, and different at different stages of our lives. Professor Melvin Kimble, Ph.D. contemporizes the profound words when he asserts, "Man does not live by welfare services and Social Security checks alone." ("Aging and the Search for Meaning" in Spiritual Maturity in the Later Years, James J. Seeber (editor), Haworth Press, 1990, p.114).

Living Life "On Purpose"

Yet where does this sense of meaning come from? Meaning comes from the subjective appraisal that your unique gifts are in fact being expressed in your life. These gifts or talents are not being expressed haphazardly, sloppily, or randomly; on the contrary, they are being focused onto a specific objective, some over-arching goal of your life that is bigger than you are. Your gifts and talents are not scattered to the four winds in confusion, they are carefully aimed and executed like an arrow deliberately drawn into the bow string, delicately aimed, and precisely released to create the full impact when it finds its mark.

Your Purpose

This bulls eye, this objective, this focused goal of your gifts and talents is called your life purpose. Your purpose, whatever it may be, is the focus of your life, the point onto which the full measure of your energy is directed. When you pursue a goal larger than yourself, when you express your giftedness to the full extent of your abilities, you are then

What Color is Your Retirement?

"harnessing the power of purpose" and consequently experiencing the health-promoting quality of enhanced life meaning.

Our cultural fear of aging, that seems so prevalent, may be the fear that our later years are simply irrelevant. This fear seems to be identifiable at younger and younger ages. I once went to a party celebrating a man's 35th birthday. The "celebration" scene was festooned with black balloons, crepe paper, a black cake, and gifts such as Geritol, Ensure, Depends, and Fasteeth. If our image of maturation is one of such decrepitude, is there any wonder that the later years have become so fearsome even for 35 year olds? Where is there room for life meaning with such a dismal perception? Yet we know that such perceptions are inaccurate. The lives of retirees are not destined to be years of decrepitude. Physical diminishment of some kind can be a part of aging, yet discovering life meaning in one's later years does not depend on our ability to perform competitive sports nor on robust physical strength. Rather, pursuing our purpose discovers meaning; it is by measuring the ways we invest ourselves in the moments of our lives (at whatever age) that makes life worth living.

Meaning does not magically materialize. Meaning already exists in our lives, but we must search for it, we must work to discover it. This discovery process is a central feature of our retirement life; it's a primal drive to find expression for the uniqueness that is our own personality. Frankl further asserts that we cannot create meaning in our lives by thought alone; our thoughts need to be energized into some form of

150

action. It seems paradoxical that on the one hand we need energy to discover our purpose, and yet on the other hand the discovery of purpose generates its own new energy.

Where We Find Meaning

So how can we discover our life purpose and find our life meaning? Dr. Kimble outlines three general areas where meaning can be garnered: 1. creative expression through achieving tasks, 2. finding goodness in our lives and 3. our approach to loss. The categorization is immensely hopeful, let's explore each of these.

Creative Expression: We are most familiar with this first source of personal meaning, pursuing goals in the form of achievements and personal productivity. Here is where we seek opportunities for creatively exercising our talents and skills. We seek to find areas and forums where we can express our unique personality traits and our developed competencies. Naturally this is a life-long quest, a search for public and private stages where we can perform, where we can show our genuine individuality. We commonly seek this expression in our professional work. We select occupations where our uniqueness can be demonstrated and exercised. We also seek to inject our uniqueness into our work every chance we can. No two people do the same job in exactly the same way; they inject their particular style, or personality into it. We choose the kind of work that "fits" us, and we shape our work to "fit" us. In doing so, we find meaning. The degree to which the genuine "you" is expressed in your work, is the same degree to which you find meaning.

Finding the Good: Kimble says that the second source of life meaning is the way we find goodness in our lives. Goodness can be found in almost everything --- in a sunset, or in a flower, in a sunny afternoon and in a rainy day, even things that appear anything but "good" can eventually lead to good. Very much good came out of World War II, even though the tragedy of the war was clearly apparent. Perhaps the most dramatic experience of goodness is in our relationships. When we can penetrate to the central core of a person, we not only have seen the "good" that is there, but we have taken one step further, we have found love. Here is the highest form of goodness and the richest source of personal life meaning on this second level.

Dealing with Loss: The third source of life meaning, according to Kimble is in our approach to loss. Here is the most hopeful source of meaning, for it is here, in the losses that life can bring, that many of us fall from hope. In his words, Dr. Kimble reminds us that, "Life potentially holds meaning up until the last breath." (p. 118). Just the other day a counselee of mine incredibly said to me, "I'm so glad I had brain cancer; if I hadn't I would have never truly understood what life is all about." He experienced meaning because he was able to transcend the scary loss in his life and focus instead upon the life transforming qualities that emerged as a consequence of his cancer. He claims that he never loved his wife quite like he does now. He describes that his life was formerly a forum for competition; a place with only one goal and that was to win. Now he sees his life through quite different eyes as a place where he can exercise his gifts and bring happiness to others.

He remains happy even though he clearly faces the real possibility that his brain cancer could reappear anytime. He reports a new richness in his life to which he was formerly blind.

The Ten Characteristics of Personal Purpose

How do we really know the degree to which we have discovered personal purpose in our lives? The average mature person might not have clarified their own personal purpose in concrete terms, yet it's generally there, it just needs to be recognized. Here are ten characteristics of persons who have high-level personal purpose. How do these apply to your life?

1. Live a meaningful life. Personal meaning in life is an intangible quality that's very hard to measure; it must be felt. Yet your subjective appraisal of the amount of personal meaning in your life is a good indicator of the presence of a personal purpose in your life.

2. Know where you are going. Personal direction comes from feeling that you have a personal mission, a cause, and a dream.

3. Be able to answer the "big question" in life such as "What's the purpose of life?" "Where am I heading in life?" "What is my goal in life?" etc.

4. Have dreams. These personal objectives are your dreams, and hopes that provide the "glue" holding you together.

5. Believe that change brings added meaning to life. Don't be afraid of change. Embrace change as the central wellspring of growth and personal development. "Flow" and bend and be flexible in the face of change. Anticipate change and adjust your life in preparation for these changes even before they come along.

6. Feel your inner energy. This energy may not be of a physical type, on the contrary you may be physically tired, yet you have an inner "life force" which ushers in a determination of mind and commitment of spirit which energizes you regardless of the physical condition of your body.

7. Engage your imagination. Imagination is not the sole province of children. Engage in lively imagination, creative insight, and prayerful meditations.

8. Feel you are part of a larger whole. Mature adults with strong personal purpose know that their presence here on this earth is intentional.

9. Experience an advancing spirituality that becomes increasingly contemplative. Interact in fellowship, yet find quiet times where you simply focus on the awe and wonder of life itself.

10. Maintain vision. Mature adults with purpose can see beyond the material plane that is in front of them. They are able to experience a fourth dimension: the spiritual dimension.

Chapter Nineteen

Education

Learning new things promotes health and well-being. When we learn new things we stimulate ourselves and not only sharpen our intellectual capacities, but our emotional and psychological strengths as well. Education is said to keep us young; using our brain showers us with health-giving energy that revitalizes us. The modern adage "use it, or lose it" may sum-up our need to remain mentally active. Your score, red, yellow, or green on the Life Options Profile, gives you a good indication of your level of interest in education.

The notion some people have of retirement as a luminous state of being next to nirvana is quickly dispelled when they actually make the transition. They may find that once the honeymoon phase is over they again fall into a routine bordering on boredom. One man asked another, *"Stan, how's the retirement going?"* To which Stan replied, *"Well, once I accompany the wife to the grocery store, watch the midday news, walk the dog, and take my nap, it's already time for happy hour. It's going OK I guess.*" Here's a life in need of a bit of stimulation. What makes it all the more tragic is that Stan is a bright guy, a guy who in his active working years was respected as a person of substance and action. What's happened to Stan? Somehow he lost is verve, lost his vitality.

Personal education in an area of interest can turn an otherwise lifeless retirement lifestyle into a vibrant and satisfying endeavor. Education has the power to fill the void that too many retirees experience. Academic and practical educational programs for lifelong learning have burgeoned over recent years. These programs offer opportunities for personal enrichment and stimulation. Education can rekindle that yearning you had in your heart and soul so many years ago. It offers a rejuvenation of soul that few things can. It provides learning challenges that unearth personal strengths and talents long forgotten or repressed.

Colleges and universities typically encourage "lifelong learners," as retirees are often called, to return to campus. Some retirees even pursue a degree, certificate, or other designation that may assist them in shifting gears into a new line of work. For most retirees however, education is not an avenue to new work, rather it's a quiet, personal, internal focusing on one's interior. Retirees find educational experiences simply for the joy of learning. Lifelong education can be many things to many different people, but essentially lifelong education speaks to that which is most noble in you, the creative in you, even the contemplative in you.

Here are some reasons why retirees seek education:

- Gives me a passion
- Stimulates new interests
- Keeps me involved
- Allows me to meet new, and interesting people
- Fills my time
- Exercises my brain
- Gives me a reason to get dressed-up in the morning
- Keeps me alive
- Fights monotony
- Lets me delve into what I wanted to in my youth
- Offers new perspectives on living well

On Line Learning

There's a revolution of learning opportunities that's cascading over the Internet. Hundreds of learning institutions, public and private universities, colleges of all types, proprietary schools of every description have found a home on the web. Some of these on-line programs offer degrees, right up to the distinguished Ph.D. Certainly there are the charlatans, but the majority of these schools are more than reputable, some are the most prestigious educational institutions in the country. You can hardly miss them; they are all over the web. Our list of resources below gives you a good place to start your search.

Several of the websites listed are clearing houses for educational programs.

www.DirectoryofonlineSchools.com

www.uwex.edu/disted/

www.detc.org

www.usdla.org

www.adec.edu

Some Internet-based programs are exclusively confined to your computer; some are interactive to varying degrees, some are called telecourses, you attend class over the telephone.

You can even combine education with travel, or eco-tourism. One interesting and well-established program is called Elderhostel. Elderhostel offers perhaps the widest variety of classes given at a vast number of sites. The courses are generally taught by retirees themselves and represent the broadest cross section of interest, depth, location, and diversity available today. Check our their website www.elderhostel.org.

Chapter Twenty

Volunteering

Medical researchers are now finding clinical proof for what most of us were taught in our youth, that giving to others is actually a form of receiving. This of course is a paradox, an apparent contradiction that points to a truth. Not only are scientists proving this paradox to be true, they further assert that helping others is good for your health.

Examples of the energizing effect of volunteering abound in medical journals. A study done at the University of Michigan revealed that persons who regularly volunteer their time heighten their overall zest for living and increase their life expectancy. Studies on the aging process have reached a similar conclusion. People who directly assist others, who share themselves openly, are healthier, happier, live longer and lead more productive lives.

What Color is Your Retirement?

The need for connection seems to be a central ingredient in our internal health-promotion system. Stress researchers Maddi and Kobasi from the University of Illinois found that persons who feel connected with other people are calmer and less worried. (The Hardy Executive: Health Under Stress, Dow Jones Irwin, Homewood, IL, 1984). Somehow it seems that when we share ourselves with others, internal mechanisms still not completely understood by modern science become activated in a positive direction. This notion takes on clarity when we remember that alienation makes us feel left out, and it provokes, fear, tension, and anxiety, all of which hasten aging.

Giving to others, of course, can take almost an infinite variety of forms, from folding sheets at the local hospital, to an understanding nod of acceptance, to empathy, compassion, and many, many different acts of service. Whatever form your volunteering takes, the core is still the same – giving of our self is offering the spirit of personal uniqueness to others. This spirit is the only gift that multiplies the more you give it away.

This uniqueness that is yours alone operates beyond the usual rules of the world, for it is by giving this uniqueness to others that we can truly appreciate what we ourselves have been given. We depreciate our self and lose sight of who we are, and what we are, when we lose our grip on our personal uniqueness. When we refuse to give our talents and gifts away, we cut ourselves off from the vitalizing channels connecting us with others, and disconnect with our own self in the process.

Attitudes

At the core of our willingness to volunteer lie our attitudes, values, and beliefs about our role and function here on this earth. What are retired persons supposed to do? So many do give of themselves, they volunteer both formally and informally, in so many endeavors that allow them to thrive. Many others however, remain unmotivated; they develop no new roles to replace former roles of wage earner, homemaker, parent, or spouse. In the absence of a productive role choice, these retirees can lapse into the most passive and unproductive role, that of a medical patient. Failing to develop an attitude of giving, they retreat to a mentality of entitlement. Their focus in life turns away from "what can I give?" and contorts into "what can I get?"

The same retirees who encourage younger persons to set goals and make life decisions, may themselves not be following the same advice in their retirement years. These unfortunate retirees somehow believe that they have "done their thing" and now it's time for rest. Leisure time does occupy a more central place in the life structure of a retiree, but when life becomes simply a pursuit of leisure devoid of focus, the benefits accrued by the increased leisure become lost in the myopic quest for diversion and even self-indulgence. Such a retirement lifestyle detracts from health, saps energy, and renders these retirees vulnerable to sickness.

Helping others appears to do the opposite. It strengthens and completes rather than weakens and fragments. Giving of ourselves enables us to recognize and be grateful for the spirit that lies within us. Such a positive attitude has a direct impact upon the chemistry in our bodies and allows us to realize ever more clearly the central life-sustaining fact of our existence. We are people of togetherness, it appears that we need each other to stay healthy, happy, and whole. Retirees moving toward youthfulness (agelessness) strive to give, and in doing so they live to their fullest potential.

One study on volunteers really brings home its value. Researchers asked volunteers how they feel when they give of themselves. Respondents gave six categories of responses to this question. They said that when they volunteered, they felt: 1) euphoric (good), 2) stronger and more energetic, 3) warmer, 4) calmer and less depressed, 5) had greater self-worth, and 6) had fewer aches and pains. Further they were asked how long they felt these feelings. Their answer was astounding; some said they felt this way just for the time they were actually doing the volunteering, others said they felt this good feeling all day, but by far the largest group said that they experienced all these wonderful feelings every time they even remembered what they had done. Wouldn't you like your medicine to work like this?

For 15 years I taught medical resident physicians the "art" (as opposed to the science) of medicine. I taught such things as communication skills, family dynamics, motivation, and many other psychosocial factors that can affect sickness. After I learned the therapeutic value of volunteering on the health of the patient, I always taught the resident to say one thing just before the patient left the exam room. I encouraged the physician to say to the patient, "*Remember to help someone today."* The benefits of volunteering are that direct; unquestionably volunteering makes you better!

Volunteering keeps you "in the loop" in your retirement years; it keeps you connected to the vital energies of the community and consequently allows you to feel useful and productive. Volunteering is clearly on the upswing in our culture; certainly among retirees this is true. Those retirees who volunteer regularly register much higher levels of life satisfaction and sense of personal meaning ... join them.

Tips for Volunteering Wisely modified from www.networkforgood.org

1) Research the causes or issues important to you. Look for a group that works with issues about which you feel strongly.
2) Consider the skills you have to offer. If you enjoy outdoor work, have a knack for teaching, or just enjoy interacting with people, you may want to look for volunteer work that would incorporate these, or other aspects of your unique personality.
3) Perhaps you would like to learn a new skill or gain exposure to a new situation. Consider seeking a volunteer opportunity where you'll learn something new.
4) Combine your goals. Look for volunteer opportunities that will also help you achieve your other goals for life. If you want to lose a few extra pounds, pick an active volunteer opportunity such as cleaning a park or working with kids.

5) <u>Don't over commit your schedule</u>. Make sure that your volunteer hours comfortably fit into an overall lifestyle schedule that suits you.

6) Nonprofit volunteer sites might have questions for you. Most nonprofit organizations that actively recruit volunteers will generally want to interview you. In a sense, you are representing them. They have big jobs to perform and they need to make sure that you have both the temperament and the necessary skill base for what makes sense for them.

7) <u>Consider volunteering as a couple, or even as a family</u>. Perhaps you can find a volunteer site where you can bring your adult children or your grandchildren; perhaps you'd like to bring a friend or neighbor.

8) Virtual volunteering. If you have computer Internet access you may find some organizations that can use your computer skills.

9) Cast a wider net; consider volunteer sites beyond the norm. Have you ever thought of day care centers, halfway houses, drug rehabilitation centers, soup kitchens and church pantries, prisons, youth organizations, sports teams, after school programs, shelters for children, children camps, and nearby parks.

Resources

Life Meaning/Spirituality

Senior Adult Ministry
http://www.senioradultministry.com/
Dedicated to the faith development needs of adults in all
Christian denominations in the second half of life

BeliefNet
http://www.beliefnet.org/
A spiritual approach to your daily health and happiness

Retirement With a Purpose > Spiritual Growth
http://www.retirementwithapurpose.com/growth/

Education

Elderhostel
http://www.elderhostel.org/
Adventures in life-long learning

Osher Lifelong Learning Institute (OLLI)
http://www.learnmore.duke.edu/olli/ (one of 70+ program
websites)
OLLI is an independent, non-profit organization, affiliated with
70+ universities and lifelong-learning institutes in the United
States supported by the Bernard Osher Foundation.

Volunteering

VolunteerMatch
http://www.volunteermatch.org/
Where volunteering begins

What Color is Your Retirement?

Experience Corps
http://www.experiencecorps.org/
New adventures in service for Americans over 55

Habitat for Humanity
http://www.habitat.org/

United Way
www.unitedway.org
Click on the "Volunteer" button to find positions in your area

Hands on Network
www.handsonnetwork.org
Click on "Find Out More" under "Volunteers" for links to
local groups with volunteer opportunities

Next Chapter Initiative
www.civicventures.org/nextchapter
Click on "Directory" for Next Chapter centers across the
country, many of which offer retirees guidance on volunteering

GENERAL RESOURCES

Aging Hipsters
http://www.aginghipsters.com/
The baby boomer generation – trends, research, comments and discussions.

Go60.com
http://www.go60.com/
Seniors aging well, wisely and successfully

Third Age
http://www.thirdage.com/
Midlife health, relationships career advice and more

2Young2Retire
http://www.2young2retire.com/
Retirement planning for people who aren't calling it quits

CARP – Canada's association for the 50 plus
http://www.carp.ca/
CARP is Canada's leading advocacy group for Canadians over 50

What Color is Your Retirement?

EPILOGUE

Retirement is supposed to be a challenging stage of life. Among other things, the bodily functions upon which we formerly relied no longer respond with the same speed, strength, and grace that they once did. But our internal resources are not gone; they're just rearranged. Where there was strength, determination now appears. Where speed once carried the day, now thoughtful understanding wins it. Where once sensory sharpness gave us an edge, now patience and wisdom provide us with sustaining power. Your retirement is like your life ... it's what you make it. Invest little and receive little ... invest a lot and find your life.

The current generation of persons preparing for life after they leave their former full-time active work, are now beginning to set the standard for what retirement will become in our culture. Will retirement remain what it has been for so many before you, a time for the pursuit of diversion, or will a new retirement emerge when and where people seek to become ever more who they truly are ... filled with vitality of mind, verve of spirit and vigor of passion? You will craft your own retirement, but you will also be setting the stage for generations behind you.